VENEERING
ESSENTIALS

SIMPLE TECHNIQUES & PRACTICAL PROJECTS FOR TODAY'S WOODWORKER

STEVEN DER-GARABEDIAN

CEDAR LANE PRESS

Publisher: Paul McGahren
Editor: Kerri Grzybicki
Designer: Lindsay Hess
Layout Designer and Illustrator: Jodie Delohery
Photographer: Steven Der-Garabedian
Indexer: Jay Kreider

Cedar Lane Press
PO Box 5424
Lancaster, PA 17606-5424

Paperback ISBN: 978-1-950934-01-0
ePub ISBN: 978-1-950934-04-1

Library of Congress Control Number: 2020948938

Printed in The United States of America

10 9 8 7 6 5 4 3 2 1

Note: The following list contains names used in *Veneering Essentials* that may be registered with the United States Copyright Office: 3M (Scotch, Scotch Performance Green Masking Tape 233+); Acmos Chemicals (Waxilit); Bessey Tools; Black Walnut Studio; CMT; Crescent Tools (Nicholson Super-Shear); Festool (DOMINO); Freud Tools; Gramercy Tools; Hold-Heet; James Bond; James Krenov; Johnson Level; Lee Valley (Chestnutt Tools); Norm Abram (New Yankee Workshop); North American Plywood Corporation of California (Wiggle Wood®); Old Brown Glue; RH Products Co., Inc. (HH-66); Roarockit Skateboard Company (Thin Air Press); Rosewood Studio; Sharpie; STAEDTLER (Mars); Starbond; Titebond (II, III, Cold Press for Veneer, Genuine Hide Glue, Original); Unibond One; VacuPress Vacuum Pressing Systems, Inc. (Compact 300, Unibond 800, Unibond One, VacuPress); Veritas; Woodstock International Inc. (Shop Fox).

To learn more about Cedar Lane Press books, or to find a retailer near you, email *info@cedarlanepress.com* or visit us at *www.cedarlanepress.com*.

DEDICATION

To Kim. Also, I love you.

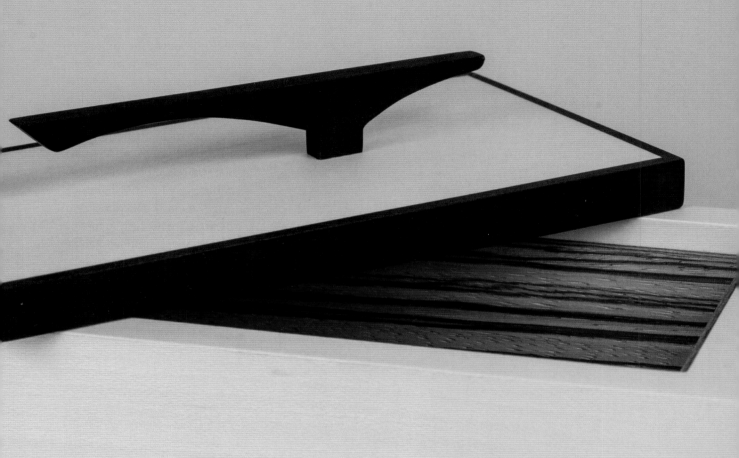

FOREWORD

Steve and I have known each other for years. We both attended Rosewood Studio (though in different cohorts), where we learned the same curriculum and studied under some of North America's top furniture makers. We studied veneering, and while I enjoy it, Steve completely fell in love with the technique. That love for veneer has influenced his work and he has truly mastered its use.

We have worked together many times over the years, including teaching together at various Canadian woodworking shows. We are known as the Vic and Steve Show—while sharing a stage to teach together, hilarity often ensues. We both enjoy educating and share a desire to pass on what we know so that all these woodworking skills don't disappear. The best part about working with Steve is that I learn something new about veneering every time. He does things differently than I do, which challenges my techniques, encourages me to grow as a woodworker, and makes me think about how I do things in my shop.

Steve is a talented designer, woodworker, and furniture maker, and the woodworking world is better for having him in it. He is a laid-back guy with a passion for teaching that comes across in his many magazine articles, seminars, webinars, private instruction, and, lucky for you, in the pages you're about to read.

There is a lot of not-so-accurate information out there in the world of woodworking. Some of these pieces of bad information are simply passed on over the years with no one testing them out to see if they are true or not. What makes Steve a great woodworker and teacher is that he isn't afraid to try different things to learn for himself. Through trial and error, he figures out what works and what doesn't so that all the techniques he teaches are successful.

The book you hold in your hands represents many years of veneering experience. While many books gloss over the basics to get to the complicated and showy stuff, Steve makes sure you, the reader, have a solid foundation prior to moving forward. He has dedicated many hours to veneering—both crafting and teaching—which you get to benefit from. So, are you excited? I'm excited for you!

Enjoy his book and prepare to learn all about veneering and how to incorporate it into your woodworking. Steve is a talented craftsman and a motivational instructor, and I'm proud to call him my friend.

Vic Tesolin,
Woodworker and author

CONTENTS

CHAPTER 1

VENEER

It's Thin and It's Real

I love veneering. I think it's a wonderful way of woodworking. It wasn't always this way. Like a lot of people, I had negative thoughts about veneering and its place in the craft of woodworking. However, during my formal schooling at Rosewood Studio, there were two moments that really opened my eyes. The first was when I realized what "sharp" truly was and how to get there. The second, well, that's when I was introduced to veneering and bending wood. I was a changed man.

My first official client—by "official" I mean not a family member—was a woman who wanted a small table. She told me she had hired me because she wanted a real wood table and, in her words, "not that fake veneered stuff." As fate would have it, the design for the piece lent itself to being veneered because the tabletop needed to be permanently attached to the apron and legs. Since I was smitten with veneering, I decided to take a chance.

Upon delivering the table, I told her that I had veneered parts of it. She didn't believe me and had to touch the table once more while taking a closer look. She must have been happy because the check wasn't canceled. In fact, she commissioned me for another piece down the road.

While you can buy "fake stuff," the veneer we are going to be using is absolutely real. It may be thin, but it is very real. And, it's only thin until you attach it to a thicker piece of plywood or other substrate.

THE SKINNY ON VENEERING

Welcome to the versatile world of veneering! Though we will go into greater detail throughout the rest of the book (as well as explaining in the rest of this chapter what you can veneer and why you should), I want to start you off on the basics. At heart, veneering is fairly simple—you need a substrate (what the veneer is attached to), veneer (the pretty face of your piece), glue (how you attach it), and pressure (to keep everything in place while the glue sets). Each of those four elements can be manipulated, and other components added to the mix, to create some pretty neat projects.

Veneer can be store bought or home-made; rotary cut or flat sliced in various ways; and made of any wood species from the plainest to the most exotic. It can be book matched, slip matched, joined into bigger sheets, or sliced into edging. You can adhere it with white glue, yellow glue, hot hide glue, or specialty veneer glues—you can even apply glue ahead of time, let it dry, and then iron it to reactivate the glue and adhere it to the substrate. Glue veneer to substrates of metal, MDF, or plywood using clamps, tape, presses, vacuum bags, or whatever weights (or heavy books!) you have around the house.

The General Steps of Veneering

A Substrate: Prepare the substrate by cutting it to size. **B** Veneer: Prepare the veneer by softening and flattening it, if needed. If your project requires a larger piece of veneer, you'll create a straight and flat joint by removing any bumps on the edges to be joined; use blue masking tape to temporarily hold the joint on the glue side of the veneer, then apply veneer tape to the show side. **C** Glue: If the glue you're using needs to be mixed or heated, do so. Apply the glue using the appropriate tools: hot hide glue is brushed on and then hammered (squeegeed); most other glues are squeezed or spread on, then rolled out with a brayer. **D** Pressure: Apply the veneer and add pressure with whatever sort of clamps or pressing you prefer. Add cauls that spread pressure to specific directions, angles, and curves as needed. Note that any assembled panels that are glued up flat or under vacuum will need to have complete air circulation around them for 24 hours to fully dry.

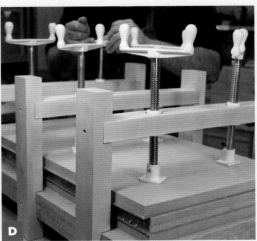

How to Use This Book

Now that you've got the basics under your belt, here's what you'll discover in the rest of the book. Chapter 1 continues to explain what veneer is. Looking for more info on substrates, types of veneer, general rules to follow, and other special considerations? Give Chapter 2 a try. As you can imagine, glue is a make-or-break element of veneering. For all the detail you want (and more!), check out Chapter 3. For more about tools you'll need, see Chapter 4—there's also a list on page 57. Visit the glossary (page 180) for terminology definitions. Use resources (page 189) to locate specific tools and materials you might find useful in your exploits.

The projects themselves walk you through a progression of veneering lessons. We'll start off simple by making iron-on veneer for a magnetic message board (page 58). Explore hammer veneering and hide glue with a nifty side table (page 72). After all that practice with normal clamps, craft your very own six-screw veneer press (page 90) and put it to use creating a divided box and tray combo that utilizes solid edging (page 100). Next is the exciting universe of vacuum pressing! With the assistance of Mother Nature and atmospheric pressure via a user-friendly kit, we'll veneer a high-contrast holly and ebony box (page 120). The last project highlights the versatility of veneer as we harness vacuum pressure with a robust pump and bag to make a curved wall panel (page 148).

Each project has measured drawings and a list of materials and tools you'll need. The cut list shows final dimensions of all components that must be a certain size. Keep in mind that veneer is easier to trim down—so start with a slightly larger piece than needed. **NOTE** In cut lists, if there are two parts that differ only by one measurement, such as a substrate and veneer face (thickness, in this case), they are shown in a single line with the differences in parentheses. Other measurements in that line without a parenthetical option are the same for both parts.

While I've given details about what I've used, change the sizes and wood choices to your preference. These are your projects and they should reflect your preferences. I would love to see your versions of projects and hear about them. Please feel free to drop me an email (*www.veneeringessentials.com* or *info@blackwalnutstudio.ca*) and a picture showing what you came up with. Have fun!

VENEER NEEDS BETTER PR

Veneering has suffered some negativity over the years, from woodworkers who see a difficult process requiring specialty tools, to the clients who see it as the mark of an inferior product. Quite the opposite is true, and I believe, like a lot of things looked down upon, veneer's plight is simply due to a lack of knowledge or understanding. Its reputation is certainly not helped by the cheap, mass-produced furniture flooding the market that trades quality in exchange for an increased bottom line. In truth, expensive, high-end furniture is usually veneered. It's a timeworn process that dates back to ancient and medieval times when pieces were handcrafted for pharaohs and royalty.

If you search the Internet for "the definition of veneer," this is what you'll get:

ve·neer
> noun
>> 1. *a thin decorative covering of fine wood applied to a coarser wood or other material.*
> verb
>> 1. *cover (something) with a decorative layer of fine wood.*

Nowhere in the definition does it say "fake," "not real," or anything negative for that matter. This is a good place to start; a positive note. It is thin, I'll give you that, but that makes it easier to carry.

WHY SHOULD WE VENEER?

There are many good reasons to integrate veneer into your woodworking. "What about special tools and adhesives and all that stuff?" you might ask. Take a quick look at the project in Chapter 5 (page 58), then come back. Chances are you've got some Titebond Original Yellow Glue and a clothes iron hanging around. If not, you'll be able to pick them both up for about $30. That project ended up costing less than $25 in materials.

So Many Beautiful Wood Options

A big reason to veneer is the access to an expanded variety of premium wood choices. When lumber gets sorted, a large portion of the best pieces are sent off to be turned into veneer. Why? With veneer, more revenue can be squeezed out of a single piece. Not only can you buy all the essential woods you normally get as solid timbers, but with veneer you can access highly figured and rare, exotic woods, including those solid pieces like burls that would be a nightmare to work with.

Less Expensive

If you had to purchase planks of that figured or rare exotic wood, it would blow your materials budget out of the water. Veneer can significantly extend your resources and allow you to work with woods you never would have before.

My tool box has survived over the years because it was made with veneer.

Better for the Environment

I'm not getting political here, just doing the math. One plank can yield plenty of veneers, yet only a few solid pieces. And, there's little waste because a veneering blade produces no kerf, like a roll of salami at the deli counter. And, as some wood species start to disappear, veneering can stretch the supply much farther into the future.

Eliminates Wood Movement

One of the primary reasons that I like to veneer is the virtual elimination of wood movement. I still work with solid lumber, but my preference is veneering, hands down. If we glue veneer to a substrate such as plywood, which is made up of multiple thin layers with glue in between each layer—well, you see where I'm going. Glue is stronger than wood: solid as a rock, with minimal movement. My tool box is a perfect example. I've dropped it twice so far, and if the back veneered panel wasn't glued into position, the box would have broken apart. Since veneer is stable and we attach it to stable substrates, it is not susceptible to warping, splitting, or even seasonal movement.

Easy to Work With

Did I mention that it's easy to carry? It's not difficult to join two or more pieces. Repairs are simple and mostly undetectable once completed. If you use hot hide glue and hammer-veneer a panel, the process can be reversed. You can create amazing designs that, if done with solid wood, would fail or fall apart due to wood movement.

WHAT ABOUT THE CONS?

So, is it all positive? One popular con regarding veneer is that it's thin, so you have to take care when handling it. Since I don't bang my lumber all over my shop—even solid timber gets damaged—I don't see this as a negative. But, yes, if you handle veneer carefully, you won't have to spend time repairing nicks and dings when you've finished your project.

Other arguments against veneer are that it delaminates, the edges get easily damaged, blistering can occur, and, when cleaning, it's easy to sand through. While these are issues, I believe they are more prone to mass-produced items and shoddy work. Proper techniques, good materials, and attention can put these deterrents to rest. The use of good substrates, proper adhesives, and care by the woodworker will ultimately lead to beautiful, stable, long-lasting furniture. Fine,

I'll admit that repairs are easier with solid timbers on things like scratches, dents, and the dreaded drink rings. In the end, I think the benefits and the joy of working with veneer will far outweigh any negatives.

KEEP IT SIMPLE

I hope by working through this book, you'll discover for yourself how easy and wonderful a method of woodworking veneering truly is. And part of succeeding is to give yourself every opportunity to do good work. If you succeed early on, you'll have the confidence and be encouraged to proceed further. With that in mind, we will keep things as simple as possible.

There is a quote by Antoine de Saint-Exupéry that when translated reads, "In anything at all, perfection is finally attained not when there is no longer anything to add, but when there is no longer anything to take away."

When I first came out of school, I would create all sorts of difficult designs with difficult joinery. I've discovered over the years that wood is beautiful on its own. I like to keep things simple in both methods and designs. I hope that translates well into your understanding of veneering.

GIVE IT A SHOT

The following chapters will give you what I think is all the information on tools and materials you need as well as good, fundemental techniques to create with this amazing medium. The methods covered are both the tried and true as well as the new. If you are unsure about a technique, grab an inexpensive piece of veneer and substrate and give it a shot. Try it before working on larger and more expensive species. Practice really does make perfect. While this book is aimed at those who have never tried veneering and are curious or those who have tried with limited success, I hope everyone who reads it might pick up a trick or two. Personally, I never want to stop learning. When I teach, I inevitably learn something as well. One of my goals in writing this book was to learn. Talking with some of the knowledgeable people in our field about veneering, I certainly achieved that. We woodworkers are a rather small community and we will become better by sharing. Let's get started...

THE PROS AND CONS OF VENEER

Pros

- Almost all the best logs are turned into veneer
- Seasonal wood movement is virtually eliminated
- Much easier to work with difficult woods as veneers, e.g., burls
- Interesting and difficult designs possible with veneer are not possible with solid wood due to wood movement
- Extends our natural resources
- Easier to create curved and bent designs
- Minimal waste when logs are turned into veneer
- Less expensive to purchase a sheet of veneer rather than a whole plank of solid wood
- Veneering over strong, stable substrates like plywood strengthens the finished piece
- It's incredibly fun!

Cons

- Certain repairs are easier with solid wood
- It's thin and must be handled with care
- Easier to sand through to the substrate or core
- Might need to purchase some new tools (though this could be a "pro" to some woodworkers.)

CHAPTER 2

A THING OR TWO ABOUT VENEERS

What Lies Underneath and What's What

There are many, many different types of veneers, ranging from those sold in big box hardware stores to those found at specialty wood retailers. For the more adventurous, there are homemade, shop-sawn veneers. In this book, all of the projects were completed with raw, unfinished commercial veneers. By raw, I mean veneers backed neither with paper nor iron-on adhesives. While those types of veneer would work fine, I find their selection to be rather plain and dull. (However, we are going to make our own iron-on veneer in Chapter 5, page 58.) In the end, we're going to have much more fun with the veneers from either brick and mortar or online specialty wood shops. For a list of potential sources of veneer and hard-to-find items, visit page 189.

HOW VENEERS ARE CUT

The methods and techniques of preparing and cutting veneers have improved over the years. A visit to a veneer mill is an excellent way to research this further, but generally, after logs are selected and prepped, there are four methods used for cutting veneers:

Rotary Cut

Rotary cutting is much like paper towels being pulled off a roll. Rotary-cut veneers are exceptionally wide and usually end up becoming the top layers of plywood.

Flat Cut

Flat cutting, or plain cutting, is when the half-log is placed heart side against the blade and sliced parallel to the grain through the length of the log. This process results in cathedral patterns.

Quarter Cut

Quarter cuts are completed with the knife at right angles to the growth rings. It produces both straight and varied lines depending on the species. In oak, it highlights the medullary rays.

Rift Cut

Rift cuts are done at a shallow angle to the radius and also result in straight-striped grain, but reduce the rays in specific woods.

When veneer is flat, quarter, or rift cut, the pieces are kept in the same sequence that they were cut off the log. This is called a flitch. When

Different Cuts for Veneer

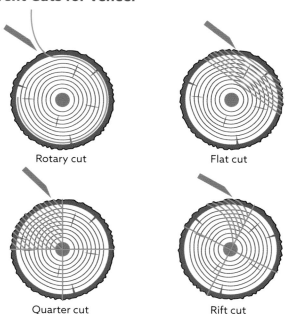

Rotary cut

Flat cut

Quarter cut

Rift cut

buying veneer or looking through it in person, it's essential to keep the flitch in order because the 1st and 2nd sheets cut in the process will match more closely than the 1st and 23rd sheets. This is important when arranging veneers for your project, especially if book matching.

SHOP-SAWN VENEERS

For those who want to experience the process of making their own veneer, shop-sawn veneers can be cut on your own bandsaw. We'll cover them again briefly at the end of the book in the afterword (page 179), but shop-sawn veneers typically require a finely tuned bandsaw, a thickness planer, and a drum sander. I used to make my own years ago, but today it is far easier to choose from the vast selection of commercial veneers.

VENEER MATCHING

Book matching is when two sequential sheets of veneer are laid side-by-side like an opened book to become a mirror image of each other.

Slip matching is when consecutive sheets are laid and joined beside each other to create a repeating grain pattern. One of the nuances of veneer is that you'll have one side that reflects light a different way than the opposite side. While a good finish will lessen the effect, slip matching can eliminate this little quirk.

As your veneering confidence increases, you can explore four-way book matches, spin matches, and other matches that create starburst patterns or radiant tabletops. Play with some veneer and take a look at some of the patterns that can be created with certain arrangements.

Book Matching

Double Book Matching

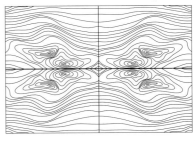

Slip Matching

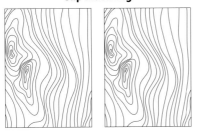

Spin Matching

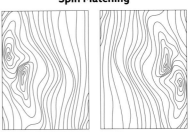

BUYING VENEERS

You can buy veneers from both local suppliers and online retailers. While it's nice to visit a supplier and select the exact pieces you want, online retailers also do a very nice job of photography and listing sizes, thicknesses, and costs. Veneers, much like solid planks that have been flat, quarter, or rift cut, will come in all ranges of widths and lengths. Some are even clipped to remove sapwood. The typical thickness will range from ⅛" or 3mm to

A variety of veneers can be found at your local wood supplier.

An in-person visit allows you to pick exactly what you need.

as thin as 1/42" or 0.6mm. Anything thicker than 1/8" I don't consider to be veneer. In fact, it will act much like solid timber as it expands and contracts with the seasons. On the other end, if the veneer is much thinner than 1/42", it's not fun at all to work with. For comparison, a piece of paper is 1/250" or 0.1mm. For the projects in this book, most of the veneers we will be dealing with will fall in the range of 1/32" to 1/42".

The important thing to remember is that, unlike solid stock that is sold by the board foot, veneers are sold by the square foot (ft²). On the cheap end, plain backer veneer used when a second layer of veneer is needed underneath the face or show veneer can cost much less than a buck. Other veneers can stretch upward in the other direction to a height that'll make you wide-eyed. The higher price points will include burls, highly figured pieces, and rare, exotic species of wood.

STORING VENEERS

When veneers are purchased and packaged, they are either flat packed or rolled and boxed. The ideal storage of veneers should be on a flat shelf. The temperature levels should be moderate, somewhere between 55 and 80° F (13 and 27° C), with the relative humidity neither too wet nor too dry, about 30% to 55%.

If your shop tends to get cold and you use a heater, a humidifier can help keep things from drying out. If your shop is in a basement, a dehumidifier can combat the dampness.

Laying veneers between two pieces of medium-density fiberboard (MDF) will work great. For most of us, space is an issue and storing long sheets of veneer flat can be a challenge. In my shop, I have a couple of dedicated shelves for veneer storage, but some are still rolled up. Always try to lay rolled veneers flat for a few days before putting them to use.

SUBSTRATES

With modern adhesives, it's possible to lay veneer onto almost everything. However, to give ourselves every opportunity to be successful with the projects, we'll be sticking with a select few that are proven. These substrates include plywood, MDF, metal, glass, and bendable plywood.

Flat-packed veneer is ready for flat storage or the next project.

Plywood

With plywood, there is a range of grades that vary in cost, quality, and thickness: construction grade, marine grade, cabinet grade, and so on. Plywood is typically made with an odd number of veneer layers. A center core is surrounded with an even number of layers on each side. It keeps things in balance, and we will too by veneering both sides when we build the projects. A favorite plywood substrate is Baltic birch. This plywood is void-free (meaning no core gaps), so it doesn't matter where we cut it. It's also constructed of many cross-laminated layers of consistent thickness with a better grade of adhesive that makes for a strong face veneer. This all leads to a stronger, stable, and better core for our veneers.

Medium Density Fiberboard (MDF)

MDF is another frequently used substrate because it has no grain, is very flat, and is easy to cut and work with. Since it has no grain, the veneer can be applied in any direction. It is also cheap and readily available in different thicknesses from ⅛" to 1", with ¼", ½", and ¾" being most common. For one of the upcoming projects, we'll glue a couple of ½"-thick pieces of MDF together to make our own 1"-thick substrate.

Metal & Glass

Metal and glass are not commonly used as substrates because they are non-porous and require a slightly different method of veneering. If you ever plan on attaching veneers to thicker pieces of metal, I would suggest using paper-backed veneer and an adhesive like Titebond II. However, to be adventurous and throw caution to the wind, we'll be making a magnetic message board using sheet metal in Chapter 5 (page 58).

Bendable Plywood

Bendable plywood goes by many names: wiggle wood, wacky wood, curve-ply, or flexply. Woodworkers who know of it, love it. Those unfamiliar with it will fall in love once they use it. Bendable plywood is made out of three layers of hardwood veneer with all the grain running in the same direction. It can be purchased in sheets sized at 4' x 8' and larger and in thickness ranging

Wiggle wood, wacky wood, whatever—by any name, bendable plywood is fun.

from 3mm to 15mm. The thinner the piece, the tighter the radius of the curve you can achieve. When buying bendable plywood, specify either long grain or short grain. (The way I remember it is to tell my supplier that I want to make either an 8' tube or a 4' tube.) In Chapter 10, we will use bendable plywood to make a form and then glue a pair of pieces together for the core on our Curved Wall Panel (page 148).

Substrates to Avoid

While it is certainly possible to veneer over solid wood, I tend to stay away from it. The thicker solid wood will expand and contract at a different rate than the very thin veneer. As a result, you'll probably see small micro-cracks develop over time. The other substrates that should be avoided are particle board, melamine, oriented strand board (OSB), and other construction-grade plywoods.

For successful veneering, we need smooth surfaces to veneer over. Any cracks, rough areas, or unevenness will show through the veneer, also known as "telegraphing," marring an otherwise beautiful surface.

Go Ahead & Experiment

When I first started exploring the landscape of veneering, I would pick up pieces of substrates and cheap veneer and experiment. I would glue them together, even the substrates that should be avoided. I tried different adhesives, different thicknesses, and so on. Not only was it fun to play mad scientist, it taught me a lot about veneering and how to work with these wonderful materials.

SOME RULES TO FOLLOW

I've been told I have a problem with authority. I spent some time with the vice-principal in high school and, later, in the office of a boss here and there. Some visits I deserved; others weren't my fault. Really! Anyway, even a self-proclaimed "rebel" like myself needs to follow some rules when veneering to achieve success. Keep them in mind in order to do your best work.

Veneer Both Sides of the Substrate

I've mentioned cross-laminating and applying veneer to both sides of a substrate. Part of what makes a successful veneer application is keeping the substrate in balance. Always remember that good plywood has an odd number of layers—a core with an even number of layers on each side. Keep this pattern going. It's very similar to applying a finish to a panel. You wouldn't finish only one side of the panel; it would warp and twist. When you attach veneer to a substrate, veneer both sides.

Grains Should Run Perpendicular

Part of what makes a better plywood stable is that each layer is stacked with its grain perpendicular to the layer underneath. In order to maintain optimum stability, that needs to continue when applying veneer. For the projects in this book, when plywood is used as a substrate, you'll see that I've cut the pieces so that the surface grain is perpendicular to the grain of the veneer. That's one of the key draws of MDF as a substrate: no grain. We can lay down our veneers in either direction.

There is an exception to this rule (shocking...a rule with an exception). When veneering over solid wood, the grain of the veneer is applied in the same direction as that of the substrate.

Glue the Harder-to-Bend Side to the Substrate, Except...

You might ask the question: What side of the veneer should be glued to the substrate? Pick up a small square of veneer and try to bend it up, then down along its grain. One side is going to feel harder to bend. I was taught that this harder side should be glued to the core.

Of course, there are always exceptions to a rule: when book matching, one piece will follow this harder-to-bend rule, but the other will not.

Use Inexpensive Backer Veneer

This can be considered a corollary to the previous rules. Take a look at the project in Chapter 10 (page 148). We need an extra layer of veneer on each face to follow the cross lamination rule. There will be times you will want to make a piece thicker to accomodate certain hardware. This is when backer veneer comes into play. No need to cover up beautiful, expensive veneer with more beautiful, expensive veneer. Use the cheap stuff. No one will see it.

EDGING & CAPPING

After we glue up our veneers to the substrate of choice, we need to cover up the edges. While the edge of Baltic birch is pleasing, it usually doesn't go with the rest of the piece—and clients don't seem to find this attractive either. In some cases, like a door or back panel, you don't have to worry about covering up the edges, because simply seating it in a groove will do the trick of hiding the edge.

Edge with Veneer or Solid Wood

There are two primary methods for covering an edge: use more veneer or use a solid wood. When using veneer, pieces are cut and glued to the edges and then smoothed at the seams for an integrated look.

If we pay close attention when applying veneer, we can continue the grain and graphics around the veneered piece. For an example, take a look at the small box project in Chapter 9 (page 120) and you'll see how the grain is wrapped around the perimeter. A very cool effect, veneered edges can be made to fall off the surface and down the sides.

Solid wood is also a good option for edging because you can select a wood that either matches or adds contrast to the veneer of the piece.

Veneer edging can provide a stylish, wrapped look to a project.

Solid wood can offer a nice contrast to your chosen veneer.

When to Edge

When do we add the veneer or solid wood edging? It might sound like a punt, but you can add it before and let the veneer cover it at the seam, or you can add it later. The choice is yours and as you learn more about veneer, it'll become clear what works best for you. Personally, I've learned to simply choose the sequence that seems the easiest.

If the solid wood is a contrasting color, then I glue it on after applying the veneer, like the box in Chapter 9 (page 120). Doing this will help to protect the veneer edges. One thing to remember if you add solid wood edging before applying the veneer: use solid wood that's ⅛" or less because if it's thicker, it could push up the veneer when it expands.

Applying and Cleaning the Edging

Typically, when edging or caps are applied, they are cut to be oversized in both width and length. This will allow for some slippage when the clamps are applied. It's very important to apply glue over the entire edge. A very strong bond is needed.

To clean up solid wood edging, place two or three layers of masking tape to prevent scratching the veneer by the edges of a block plane. Let this ride on the veneered or raw surface until the edging is just proud of flush. You can then use sandpaper the rest of the way.

To clean veneer edging, use the teeth on the side of a mill file to cut the edging almost flush to the adjacent surface. Like the block plane, wrap two or three layers of blue masking tape around the tip to avoid scratching the veneered surface. Hold the file at a slight angle away from the edge and only file toward the center; never file backwards. Sandpaper in a block will flush it up completely.

Blending the Edges Together

Whether solid wood or veneer edging is used, in both circumstances a little trick with a fine-toothed file and/or sandpaper will blend the two edges together nicely. Simply file or sand the edges toward each other at 45° angle, using a light touch. Applying a finish will conceal the edges further and, in the end, it will take a close inspection to see the seam.

Blending Veneer Edges

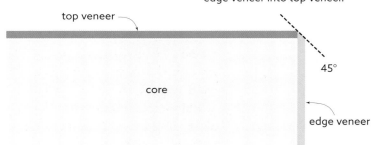

File at approximately 45° to blend edge veneer into top veneer.

top veneer

core

45°

edge veneer

A tight bond and a sharp plane make quick work of a solid wood edge.

The masking tape will help prevent scratches as you work, as well as raising the blade slightly to avoid cutting the veneer.

SANDING: NO HEAVY HANDS ALLOWED

Sanding veneer is a delicate operation—or it should be. Remember how thin it is? Stay away from belt sanders and use power sanding only for a general cleanup. Switch to hand sanding with loose sandpaper or a block sooner than later. And, when using a random-orbit sander, it's best to use a vacuum with it rather than just the bag so dust doesn't build up.

For hand sanding, you can buy a block or can make your own. Just be sure to add a piece of cork to soften the sanding face. There are even hand sanding blocks that you can connect to your vacuum. While you're at it, you can also make your own sanding sticks for blending veneer edges or veneer surfaces to solid wood edging by simply applying self-adhesive sandpaper to popsicle sticks or tongue depressors.

Remember, it's very easy to sand through veneer and into the substrate. Typically, you'll see the veneer lighten up and then immediately you will see substrate. Don't worry; this is going to happen to you. It still happens to me when I try to rush cleaning up a piece. The best practice, other than taking your time, is to only use power sanding to do general cleanup. But, if you do sand through—and can stop in time to avoid serious damage—you can easily make repairs with stain markers, permanent markers, or even lacquer sticks.

Veneer requires a light touch, like these sanding blocks with cork and other simple edge sanders.

SOFTENING

Occasionally, you are going to come across veneers that are brittle or buckled. It's usually a good idea to soften or flatten them 24–48 hours before pressing your project. If you're not sure whether the piece needs softening, one quick method will help you decide and it requires only a coin from your pocket.

Slide the coin along the veneer in question; if there are gaps of more than ⅛" between the coin and the veneer, it should be flattened or softened. While I've vacuum-pressed buckled veneer with no consequences (using water-based glues), I've found softening very useful with brittle veneer or if I'm having trouble jointing the edges. Once more, play around in the shop. Try it for yourself and see the results.

Homemade versus Commercial

When I was fresh out of school, I used to mix up my own softener with 25% denatured alcohol, 25% glycerin, and 50% water. There are all kinds of home-brew recipes out there that will work. The master woodworker Tage Frid used to make his softener with glue, flour, glycerin, alcohol, and distilled water. Lately, to make life easier, I just buy a commercial flattener at my local retailer. It's easy to apply, it's inexpensive, and it lasts a long time.

Either homemade or commercial softener will help with brittle veneer.

A softener can make brittle veneer salvageable.

You'll find a source or two for softener in the back of the book.

Applying the Softener

Follow the directions if you purchase a softener. Typically, after the softener is applied, the veneer is stacked between sheets of absorbent paper—unprinted newspaper, brown paper, or paper towels—which is then sandwiched between a couple of pieces of MDF. You'll need to change the paper when it gets soaked every few hours for the first 24 hours. Adding weight on the stack will help; after the initial softening, it can even be pressed in a vacuum bag.

With commercial formulas, the softness will last about 48 hours. The good news is that if life gets in the way and you don't get to use the veneer in that time frame, it can be softened again without consequences. In the end, with a little softener, a brittle piece of veneer that would normally crack and break apart can be rolled up like a newspaper.

CHAPTER 3

ALL ABOUT GLUE

Things Are Going to Get Sticky

There's no veneering without glue, so it is an important topic. While there are a lot of choices out there when it comes to the glues you can use, you only need one or two. Most gluing that I do is with white carpenter's glue, such as Titebond or a similar polyvinyl acetate (PVA) adhesive. Hide glue is a little more complex, but has a long history of being used for veneering. We'll explore other options and take a look at the proper procedures for gluing—including the all-important dry run.

KNOW WHAT YOU'RE GLUING

You may know everything about glue, but you may not know everything about gluing your particular project. When I first started woodworking, I would get the parts together, apply glue, and hope that it all went well. After all, 10 to 15 minutes seems like a long time—what could go wrong? Well, it is not a long time once you apply glue. Glue makes things permanent. Soon, panic mode sets in and you're reaching for more clamps that don't quite fit around the others, pulling things back apart, and adding more glue to account for all the glue that's now on your shirt and hands while trying to set it all back up. Yikes! A word of advice—you can avoid glue anxiety by doing a dry run. It is a rehearsal of sorts. A dry assembly not only tells you how many clamps you're going to need, but it also prepares you to set them at the right openings. A rehearsal is going to tell you if you need to glue the components in sections and then bring them together after the first—or the second—set has cured. Add the dry run to your process so you can practice the steps of gluing without any adhesive. Keep in mind that all time is relative: your shop is going to have different gluing times than mine or the good folks at the Titebond laboratory. So when we talk about open time, assembly time, and cure time, let's try not to overthink it. In the spirit of keeping things simple, we can agree that we're all pretty close when it comes to glue times. The open time and assembly time are going to be about 10 to 15 minutes for practically all the adhesives used in this book.

The cure time is dependent on the glue being used, but err on the side of longer rather than shorter. That said, most of the glues used on the following projects are PVAs. A PVA glue cures when the moisture evaporates, creating the bond between the pieces. So, it's pretty simple: if you have a giant fan blowing air in your shop, the cure time is going to be fast; if there is no air movement and it's humid, well, you get the idea.

POLYVINYL ACETATE (PVA)

Most woodworkers refer to PVAs as water-based glues. They include white and yellow glues; Titebond II, III, and Cold Press for Veneer; and Unibond One. They don't dry rock hard and have what is referred to as "cold creep"—which means that it remains slightly flexible. Some PVA's, such as the veneer-specific glues, will dry harder, but not as hard as the urea-based adhesives outlined later.

As mentioned, PVA glue cures when the water evaporates from the adhesive, and the two pieces of wood, such as the veneer and substrate, are tightly bonded. Obviously, there is more science to this than we can cover here. (Remember the Titebond laboratory?) We simply want to know the differences between them and how they work individually.

Both Titebond Cold Press for Veneer and Unibond One have solids added to their mixtures. This helps limit the glue from seeping through the veneer and onto the show side—referred to as bleed-through. It's a good idea to mix these glues before you use them because the solids end up on the bottom and show up as a dark band on the bottle.

Titebond III is a waterproof PVA glue that has a longer open time.

Titebond Original is a yellow glue that works very well in making your own iron-on veneer, which we'll cover in Chapter 5. The reason I like

PVA glues are a can't-do-without staple when veneering.

using the PVA glues listed here is because they can be used right out of the bottle, I don't need to wear protection because of their ingredients, and they work really well.

HIDE GLUE

Tage Frid once said that you could veneer the world with hide glue and a veneer hammer—which is true because you wouldn't need clamps. Hide glue goes way back, but, thankfully, it's still being used today. It's infamously made from animal parts, which is why its past is associated with the meat-packing and tanning industries. Nevertheless, it's a wonderful glue with reversible bonding properties that are a blessing to those in the refurbishing end of woodworking, and cleans up easily with vinegar.

The Basics of Hide Glue

Hot hide glue, not to be confused with liquid hide glue, comes in the form of small granules or pearls. To make the glue, mix cold water with the granules in a glass jar and heat the mixture up to 150° F (65° C). Refined, high-quality hide glue is not expensive and, contrary to what some folks say, it doesn't smell bad unless you heat it too high, upward of 170° F (76° C). Hide glue comes in different strengths with the stronger types having the shorter open times. A good place to start with hide glue is 192-gram strength because it works great for hammer veneering and the excess mixed glue can be refrigerated and used after re-heating it.

Just add water plus heat and you've got the perfect glue for hammer veneering.

Regarding the often-confused liquid hide glue, such as Old Brown Glue and Titebond's Genuine Hide Glue: they are best suited to joinery and not hammer veneering. But, they are still reversible with heat and moisture.

The Hesitation with Hide Glue

As great as hide glue is, I think there is a hesitance to using it. Part of the problem is trying to describe the consistency of what hide glue should be like before application. When I first started using it, I was told that I needed a syrup-like consistency. What if you live up north and have maple syrup or you live down in Florida with pancake syrup? Big difference. Let me add my 2¢ worth by saying you want a consistency of runny syrup, much runnier than you think.

Another cause for uncertainty with hide glue is how to heat it and keep the temperature consistent while using it. One solution is the Hold-Heet automatic electric glue pot. If you are going to dive into using hide glue, my suggestion is to get one. It's expensive, but it works great. There are other options, like the cosmetic wax heater that I use in Chapter 6. It's much cheaper and there are plenty of models to choose from. I borrowed this concept from Roland Johnson, who came up with the idea for heating alternatives after hearing students complain that buying a glue pot was expensive. Other creative woodworkers have used baby bottle warmers and crock pots in a double-boiler method.

The Ease & Upside of Hide Glue

Once you get past these small—but quickly solvable—issues, hide glue is really enjoyable and very easy to work with. In a nutshell, using a brush you can buy or make yourself, you apply warm hide glue to the substrate, place the veneer face down and brush on some hide glue, flip it over, and start squeegeeing it from the center out with the veneer hammer. The veneer hammer gets rid of any excess glue, cools down

To paraphrase Tage Frid, "With hide glue and a veneer hammer, you can veneer the world."

the glue to the point where it gets tacky, and the glue on the show side—collected when the veneer was first placed facedown on the substrate—acts as a lubricant while also filling any open pores. It's that easy. More details about hide glue are covered in Chapter 6 as part of the Floating Side Table project.

The best thing about hide glue is that it reminds me of my childhood days because it's sticky and messy, but there are lots of do-overs!

BEYOND THE FRIENDLY PVAS & HISTORIC HIDE GLUE

My suggestion of keeping things simple will have us sticking with the previously listed PVA adhesives and hide glue. They're easy to work with and all the projects in the book were completed with those types of glue. But, should you continue to experiment with veneer, there are several other adhesives that you'll probably come across. They each have their place in woodworking and, specifically, in veneering.

If you jump into using hide glue, a glue pot makes life easy.

A SHOP-MADE HIDE GLUE BRUSH

When I found out that the company in France that supplied my hide glue brushes closed down, I took mine apart to see about making my own. Turns out it's really simple and takes no time at all. A mop type of brush will hold hide glue and move it around the surfaces.

A I started with a piece of maple or a similar wood that's roughly 1" square and about 12" long. **B** Using a bandsaw, I cut a tapered tenon on the end with the taper running thinner back to the handle. Using spokeshaves, chisels, files, and sandpaper I refined and smoothed the shape. **C** Next,

after buying some natural bristle brushes, I took them apart and temporarily tacked them around the tapered tenon with some CA glue. Then, I wound some plain, untreated cotton cording around the bristles to lock them in place. **D** Finally, I heated up some hide glue in my antique glue pot and electric warmer and applied it to the threads, creating a shop-made hide glue brush.

If you don't feel like making your own, any glue brush will work, but it's a good idea not to include any metal in the components.

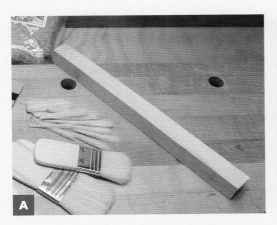

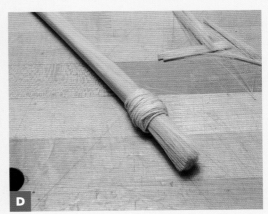

Urea Formaldehyde

Unibond 800 is a modified urea formaldehyde two-part adhesive of resin and powder. It requires a mask and goggles while mixing, but once you get past that hurdle, the application is fairly easy. Unibond 800 has a long open time and, unlike PVA glues, it dries rock hard. But, in addition to the toxicity, this glue's downside is its cost and relatively short shelf-life.

Epoxy, Contact Cement & Polyurethane

While epoxy, contact cement, and polyurethane glues can be used in veneering, they are far from my first choice. I use epoxy more for doing repairs, such as filling voids. Contact cement and polyurethane adhesives are only used when the veneer is hard or impossible to clamp. I'm also tempted to use paper-backed veneers when using these glues. I'd recommend playing around with these so you can see for yourself how they work and if they can be put to use in your shop.

Cyanoacrylate (CA)

Cyanoacrylate glue, better known as either CA or crazy glue, can be very helpful with veneer repairs. It comes in consistencies ranging from thin to thick, as well as in tints like brown and black.

After applying white glue to edging, I will often use CA glue to quickly hold it in place while the white glue cures. I'll still use clamps and cauls, but a couple of CA drops ensure that the edging doesn't shift.

Quick-drying crazy glue comes in handy for veneer repairs.

Another great use for CA is putting a small amount in screw pilot holes in MDF or plywood; this makes the walls and threads rigid for greater screw-holding power.

SPREADING THE GLUE

When veneering, you usually have a lot of area to cover with glue, so while I've been known to spread glue with my fingers, that usually doesn't work. You can buy commercially made spreaders that work really well, but they can be expensive.

Since the time I was in school, I've been using a brayer—a small hand roller from the printing industry that's used to roll ink and paint onto printing blocks. I find that it spreads the glue very evenly, and if it's washed after each job, it will last for a long time. I have a tendency to add more glue than necessary. How-ever, the brayer corrects this error by pushing the excess glue off the substrate. Inexpensive brayers can be found in many different sizes at arts and crafts retailers.

The other spreader I often use for veneer work is the notched plastic trowel that was originally made for spreading epoxy. The ⅛" notches are perfect for spreading just the right amount of glue. Any hardware store should have a good selection of notched spreaders in the paint sec-tion. In a pinch, you can make your own notches on a straight plastic spatula with a bandsaw.

Finally, for smaller work and join-ery, I like to use the brushes from Titebond and smaller versions you can find at woodworking retailers. Their glue paddles do a nice job of getting into mortises or other hard-to-reach areas.

The successful spreading of glue requires only simple and inexpensive tools.

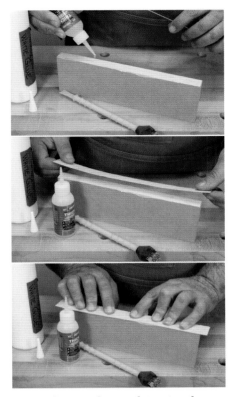

Crazy glue can keep edging in place while the PVA glue dries.

MAKE A FLYSWATTER GLUE MIXER

As mentioned, glues specifically made for the application of veneer contain solids. They prevent the glue from seeping through the thin veneer and onto the show—or face—side of the project. **A** However, if you take a look at a bottle of Titebond Cold Press for Veneer that has been sitting around for a bit, you'll see the solids in the form of a dark band at the bottom. We need to get these solids back into the mix. Sadly, the glue cannot be shaken to get it to mix; it must be stirred. (Sorry, Mr. Bond.)

B So, we could get a long thin scrap of wood, use the bottle neck as a fulcrum, and start to stir. I'm all for mixing, but I'm lazy when it comes to this kind of work. **C** We could buy a paint mixer, but the smallest and most flexible of paint mixers will barely fit into the opening of the gallon jug, never mind the smaller squeeze bottles or quart size ones. What to do?

Make Your Own

D I was at the dollar store and came across a set of two flyswatters for $1.25. **E** They were perfectly perforated, but slightly larger than what I needed, so I used a knife to cut the plastic ends to shape. **F** After wrapping tape around the metal arm just below the handle, I used wire cutters to snip off the handle. **G** I could now chuck the new glue mixer into my drill. **H** The mixer fit perfectly into the squeeze sized bottles. **I** You can see the difference between the non-mixed glue on the right and the freshly mixed on the left. What was that saying about "where there's a will..."?

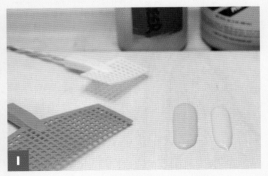

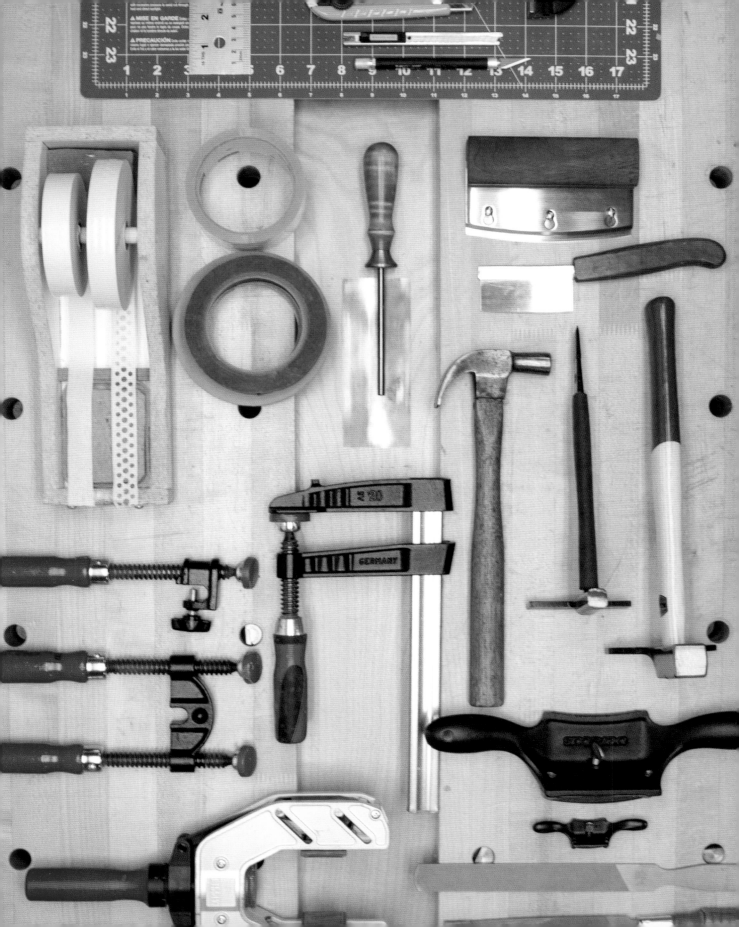

CHAPTER 4

THE TOOLS YOU'LL NEED

Some, You Might Even Make

We all love tools. If there's an excuse to pick up a new tool—or to make one—you can count on woodworkers to be first in line. There are some really nice options in our little world of woodworking. Contrary to popular opinion, to get started in veneering you really don't need a lot of tools. But once you get started tooling around with veneer, helpful tools will pop on your radar screen left and right. Vacuum kit, anyone?

Some of the veneering tools can get pricey, so to have fun and to save a few dollars we are going to make one or two tools like the veneer tape dispenser on page 44. For a good commercial veneer tape dispenser, you'll cough up $150.00 or more.

For the rest of the tools, you'll most likely have some in the shop—such as clamps, masking tape, scissors, scrapers, and files. If you haven't done any veneering, then a veneer saw or a veneer hammer probably isn't hiding in your tool chest and you might need to purchase them. They don't have to be fancy or expensive, but try to get the best you can afford. As the saying goes, you get what you pay for—especially with woodworking tools.

(L to R) The usual tape suspects: veneer; binding; packing; and blue masking or painter's tape.

TAPE

If I knew how much tape I was going to go through when I first started woodworking—even more so for veneering—I would have bought stock in 3M. For veneering, there are three types of tape that we use constantly: blue masking (or painter's) tape, veneer tape, and clear packing tape. Binding tape is another tape that you'll use, but not as much. And when it comes to purchasing tapes for use in veneering, stick with brand names; you'll only get frustrated with generic, no-name alternatives.

Blue Masking Tape

You're going to use a lot of blue masking tape, sometimes referred to as painter's tape. It's the weakest adhesive of all the masking tapes, down the ladder from the green and the tan versions that don't have a place in veneering. In fact, sometimes you're going to find that even the blue version is too strong for certain veneers. When that happens, it can be made slightly less tacky by pulling it between your thumb and forefinger.

When peeling off blue tape from veneer, the trick is to pull it low and against itself rather than up high and away at 90°. Blue masking tape, along with a sharp blade, is also handy for getting clean cuts on veneered

When paired with a sharp blade, blue masking tape burnished to the surface will make for clean cuts.

surfaces. The trick is to burnish down the tape to the veneer using a hammer with a slightly rounded head.

Veneer Tape

Some veneer tapes have two, three, or five holes across, while others have none. There is even a seven-hole version mainly used in a mechanical veneer stitcher. The most commonly used and readily available veneer tapes are the zero- and three-hole versions.

Veneer tape holds two or more veneer pieces together while it is being glued to a substrate. It can also be used to hold a rip in the veneer together while being pressed. The idea is that masking tape is first used to hold veneer seams together on the side to be glued. When secured, the sheets are then flipped over and the veneer tape is applied. The beauty of masking tape is that it can stretch a bit, which creates a clamp that keeps the seam together when placing veneer tape on the

Masking tape creates a visible bump.

other side. With the veneer secured by veneer tape, the masking tape is peeled off when it is time to glue.

Veneer tape is gummed and must be moistened to activate the adhesive. It is also thin and therefore can be used while pressing veneers. Masking tape is too thick to be used this way because it will leave an impression on veneers. Veneer tape shrinks slightly as it dries, so you cannot stretch veneer tape because it will tear. After applying the veneer tape, you can use a warm iron to dry it out or place it between two pieces of MDF while it dries. As mentioned, leave the blue tape on the glue side until it is time to actually glue.

Veneer tape can be stacked two pieces thick before it telegraphs through the veneer. On thicker veneers, even a third layer won't show up on top. There are going to be times when you need to leave veneer tape in the pressing to be covered up permanently. Case in point is the backer veneer for the Curved Wall Panel (page 148). For instances like these, I use the three-hole tape so the glue will penetrate the holes to create wood-to-wood contact. Blank tape is much easier to remove after a pressing and will not break apart as easily. To remove veneer tape, use a wet sponge to remoisten the tape. After a half-minute or so you'll start to see the veneer tape going from white to translucent. Start peeling it off and apply more moisture if needed. For stubborn areas, use a card scraper to clean up.

MAKE A VENEER TAPE DISPENSER

It is much easier to handle tape, especially veneer tape, when it is fed from a dispenser. Since commercial versions can be costly, this will be a worthwhile and fun little project.

For the body of the dispenser, melamine (readily available in two-sided laminate) is preferable to fend off moisture and be heavy enough to stay put on the workbench. The roll is a short piece of a ½" dowel and the serrated blade is from an old hacksaw. While there are lots of ways to add moisture to the veneer tape, I cut the top off a small plastic container that fits into the dispenser and then inserted a small kitchen sponge. Simply moisten the sponge and dampen the tape before cutting off the length you need.

A In addition to the dowel and a small section of blade, you'll need five pieces of ½" melamine to make the dispenser: two sides (12" x 4"), a bottom (12" x 4"), a back (3" x 4"), and a front (1½" x 4") to hold the blade. **B** Use double-sided tape to hold the two side pieces together and draw a pleasing profile on the outside face. Cut the profile on the bandsaw, then smooth it with a spindle sander or sanding block. It's a good idea to drill the hole for the ⅜" dowel while the pieces are attached.

C Cut the back and front ends for the side pieces, with the taller piece at the back and the shorter for the front. With brad nails and glue, attach the pieces together using butt joints. Scratch the melamine with 120-grit sandpaper where it will be joined. Cut a piece for the bottom; using brad nails and glue, attach it to the dispenser. **D** Cut the hacksaw blade on a grinder to fit across the front of the dispenser. Drill a pair of holes in the blade to mount it. Position the blade with the teeth slightly higher than the front edge and mount it with a pair of round head screws. **E** Glue in a little crosspiece to hold the sponge container near the front. To stop the veneer tape from unraveling every time you pull the tape, place a sponge at the back that creates just enough friction no matter how small the roll gets. **F** Add some water to your container and you're ready to tape some veneer.

Packing Tape

Packing tape is used as a glue resister. PVA glues will not stick to it, so we apply it to cauls to make sure they do not become a permanent part of the veneer sandwich. Once more, brand-name tape works better, as the cheaper alternative only tears apart as you try to peel it off the roll.

Another product called Waxilit can also be used. It is a silica-free wax that also acts to resist glue. It can be used to cut down on friction and as a moisture barrier for cast-iron surfaces on the tablesaw and bandsaw.

Binding Tape

There is one more tape that luthiers are more apt to know but will come in handy for us as well. It is officially called Scotch Performance Green Masking Tape 233+ by 3M, but you will more often see it called binding tape. It is green, but is distinct from the green masking tape mentioned earlier. It has really good holding power but yet releases cleanly when pulled off; it is a little tougher and can be stretched tight. It works great as a clamp in situations where a true clamp is just too big or awkward to use. There have also been times where I've used this binding tape and cauls for straight runs when the edging lies down clean and my clamps are otherwise tied up on other glue-ups.

Binding tape works well as a clamp when clamps are too big or tied up on other glue-ups.

KNIVES, SAWS & SCISSORS

Believe it not, I didn't purchase a veneer saw for a very long time. I eventually broke down, but I still rarely break one out. A sharp knife does amazing work and so will a pair of sharp scissors. My favorite knife is the utility knife because the blades are stout and rigid.

Knives

In addition to the aforementioned utility knives, breakaway and scalpel-style craft knives also work well. While these blades don't leave the most ideal surface to join veneers, we can perfect them with the jointing jig and jointer sander or handplane (see page 51). Use a sacrificial piece of wood underneath your cuts. A self-healing mat available from hobby and craft stores works perfectly for this task.

When cutting veneer with knives, oftentimes the substrate will be used as the template. When trimming an edge, for instance, you will

A straightedge with some self-adhesive sandpaper will provide a guide for a clean cut.

To prevent tearing, make ¾ of the cut and then finish in reverse from the end of the cut back.

simply cut the veneer around the piece of substrate.

Another way of using a knife is to pull it along a straightedge. To help lock the straightedge in position, apply some self-adhesive sandpaper in the 120-grit range to the underside. Don't try to cut through the veneer in one pass. It's better to take multiple light passes until you break through.

When cross-cutting veneers, the veneer will tear or rip as you get close to the end of the cut. As mentioned previously, burnished blue-masking tape works well in this situation to minimize tearing. Another helpful technique is to make ¾ of the cut towards you and then cut back from the bottom up to finish.

Basic knives, scissors, a straightedge, and a self-healing mat are you need for clean, crisp cuts.

For a good clean cut, a veneer saw does a great job.

Veneer Saws

While I still tend to gravitate to my knives, veneer saws do an excellent job of cutting veneers. When used, they almost cut an ideal seam to join another piece of veneer.

There are several well-made saws that you can find at specialty retailers. One of the saws I use is from Gramercy Tools. Based on a traditional French version, it's well made and makes very crisp cuts, comes sharpened, and is easy to use because your hand is directly over the cut.

The 50 TPI veneer saw from Chestnutt Tools is also very nice to use. It too comes pre-sharpened and requires only a light touch. There are other veneer saws out there of varying quality and cost, but some will not come sharpened and require some tweaking before you can use them.

Most veneer saws come with a convex blade, which has a single bevel and a flat back. They are not meant to be used like a dovetail or tenon saw, but rather with a straightedge or straight block of wood to draw the saw against. A veneer saw can be pushed or pulled; changing the angle will allow you to use most of the teeth on the saw and stop the teeth from digging in.

Like when using a knife, you take multiple passes with a veneer saw until you cut through the veneer. Veneers can also be stacked and cut in this manner. When doing this, replace the cutting mat with a piece of plywood. A good trick to make this work smoother is to run the grain of the sacrificial plywood perpendicular to the cut.

Scissors

With tame or small sections of veneer, a pair of sharp scissors can be used to make good cuts. If the veneers are brittle or buckled, the scissors won't do a very good job. Put them away and reach for the knife or veneer saw.

VENEER HAMMERS

Veneer hammers are more like a squeegee than a hammer. They have a rounded wide tip, usually made of brass, that allows you to put a tremendous amount of pressure over a small area as you slide over the veneer. This not only forces excess hide glue out from under the veneer, but also prompts the glue to cool down, which starts the curing process.

The semi-circular edge is made of brass so it will not react to certain woods, like steel does with oak. Like all the wonderful tools needed for veneering, there are various versions on the market in a wide range of prices. If you're feeling adventurous, there are plans online to make your own.

More like a squeegee, a veneer hammer exerts tremendous pressure when gluing.

VENEER JOINTING

In a perfect world, the veneer sheets would all be as wide as the dimensions of the project. There are wide sheets for sure—I've bought black walnut veneer up to 16" wide—but chances are you're going to need to join two or more pieces of veneer together to cover the substrate. Fear not! This is not a difficult job and it's very similar to joining solid timbers. The difference is that when working with veneer, it's essential to hold down the two edges so they don't buckle as a jointer or jack plane is passed over them. MDF pieces work great for this process. In fact, you can make a dedicated jointing jig that will be ready for use all the time (see page 51).

To joint two veneer edges, place them together and then close them up like a book. Next, clamp them tightly between two pieces of MDF with no more than ¼" of the edges sticking out. **NOTE** The MDF panels are not being used as a straight-edge fence but are only holding the veneers steady as we pass our choice of cutter over the veneer edges.

Run your jack or jointer plane over the edges with a light touch. For this, I find a Krenovian-style wooden jack plane works a little better because it allows that important lighter touch.

Sometimes the grain of the veneer doesn't like to be hand-planed and the blade will chip at the edge rather than leave a clean, ready-to-be-glued edge. When this happens, you need to switch to sandpaper. There are several options

Veneer pressed between MDF can be jointed with a sharp jack, jointer plane, or sander.

when working with sandpaper. You can make a square wooden block or grab some aluminum tubing and attach sandpaper of different grits to make an effective jointing tool. You can also purchase a shooting sander that works great when your veneer is uncooperative.

While it's not imperative that the sandpaper or plane meets the edges of the veneer at 90°, it's a good idea to come as close as possible. If you are slightly off, it won't matter much. Keep going until both edges are smooth and even. Unclamp the veneers, bring the edges together, and use blue masking tape to hold them in place.

Finally, there are methods for power jointing veneers or even stacks of veneers. One technique is to close the veneers like closing a book and then use a track saw with its zero-clearance edge to cut the veneers. It's quick and easy to

Before jointing the edge, you can see the gaps between the pieces.

After closing the two veneers on each other and using sandpaper or a plane to even the edges, the angles automatically match when opened up. It's actually difficult to find the joint!

MAKE A JOINTING JIG

While any two pieces of MDF that are long and wide enough to sandwich veneer between them will work, a dedicated jig makes veneering much easier. These can be made in various lengths to suit your projects. For width, the most useful size is 24".

A Start by having the hardware on hand: two ¼"-20 x 2" hex head bolts, two 2"-long compression springs, two washers, and two matching knobs or wing nuts. Clamp the two pieces of MDF together and use an awl to mark a spot ½" in from the sides and ¾" from the top. While the panels are still clamped together, drill through with a ¹⁄₁₆" drill bit. Separate the two halves. In what will become the bottom piece, using the ¹⁄₁₆" hole as your center point, drill a ⁷⁄₁₆" hole about ³⁄₁₆" deep

into the outer surface. This will be where the hex bolt will be seated when assembled. Flip the piece over and drill a hole that is the outer diameter of your spring. This hole is only about ¼" deep. Now, working on the top piece, and using the same drill bit for the spring, drill two more holes in the underside of the top about ⅜" deep. Attach 120-grit self-adhesive sandpaper to the inside surfaces at the leading edge. **B** Make sure the hex head bolts on the bottom are seated tightly so the corners of the bolt cut into the MDF and stop it from spinning. **C** Slip the springs into position over the bolt. **D** Put the top piece of MDF over the bolts. **E** Finally, add the washers and knobs. **F** You're now ready to start jointing!

If you have a track saw with a zero-clearance edge, you can joint veneers quickly.

accomplish. This method works best if you use a blade with a negative rake angle like the blades typically made for cutting metal. There are some manufacturers, like Freud, that do make a negative rake angle blade for track saws. For added insurance, I place the veneer between two pieces of thin hardboard to act as sacrificial pieces when using a track saw.

CLAMPS

It is so true that you can never have enough clamps. And when it comes to veneering, you'll figure out a way to use most of them to hold your edging in place as the glue dries.

Cauls

Before tackling the different styles of clamps, let's talk about clamping cauls. A caul is essential for successful veneering. Cauls not only protect our precious veneered (or even solid wood) surfaces from the clamp pads, but also act to spread the clamping pressure. Clamping pressure radiates outward in a cone shape from the pad of the caul. The thicker the caul, the more pressure is applied across the surface.

When I make clamping cauls, I mostly like to use pine and, as you can see throughout this book, I cover them with blue masking tape or clear packing tape so they resist glue. Pine is the wood of choice because it is soft enough to give if

Clamping Cauls

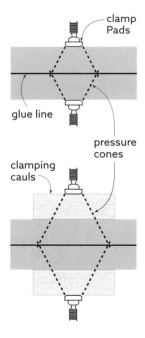

too much pressure is applied or if the surface is not as perfect as it should be. For curved surfaces such as the tea tray in Chapter 8, hardboard that is ⅛" thick works great as a caul because it can nicely match a profile if it's not too radical.

Binding Tape

The most basic of all clamps is the 3M binding tape that we discussed earlier (page 46). This handy tape can be stretched and held tight, yet still pulls off cleanly. When using binding tape, make sure to use cauls like you would for any other clamp.

Three-Way Edge Clamp

The next type is the three-way edge clamp. The two opposing clamp pads pinch the piece while the third pad pushes against the edging, holding it in place while the glue cures. These are relatively inexpensive and readily available at hardware or woodworking stores. For this style

of clamp, however, I like to make a different type of caul with sandpaper. (See the sidebar on page 54.)

Spindle Clamps

You can buy spindle clamps that attach to *F*-style clamps and work much like the three-way clamps mentioned above. In fact, it's a good idea to use the shop-made sandpaper cauls with these too.

The best and easiest-to-use edge clamps are the one-handed version from Bessey Tools. These will grip the surface and apply more than enough pressure to the caul and edging material. They do not mar the veneered surfaces and center themselves very nicely on the edge.

Classic Clamps

When gluing edges on opposite straight edges, regular *F*-style clamps, parallel clamps, or even pipe clamps will work quite nicely. In fact, if there is a slight curve, the

Clamps seen here (from left to top right): three-way edge clamp and caul, one-handed clamp, and single and double post spindle clamps that attach to a classic *F*-clamp.

MAKE A THREE-WAY EDGE CAUL

These small cauls come in handy when using a three-way edge clamp. A For ease, start with two pieces of ¾" MDF sized to the same dimensions as a sheet of sandpaper. Using glue, attach sandpaper to each piece of MDF. Place a sheet of folded wax paper between the sandpaper sides of the MDF panels and clamp them together. Each panel will act as a caul for itself. B When the glue has cured,

cut slots in the panels with the tablesaw. Raise the blade so that there is just the smallest amount of MDF left before cutting the sandpaper. C Use a utility knife to cut the rest of the way through the panel slots. D Finally, mark the center and drill holes to allow clamping pads to slip into the cauls. This creates a non-slip and non-marring clamp pad for this style of edge clamp.

A

B

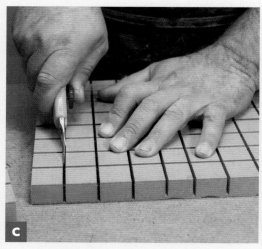

C

D

swivelling action on better *F*-style clamps will not limit the applied pressure nor slip.

TABLESAW BLADES

For the most part, a combination-style blade sits in my tablesaw. However, when I'm cutting veneer panels, I switch over to a dedicated plywood/veneer blade. They typically have 80 or more teeth with blade angles that allow for a cleaner cut in plywood as well veneered panels with MDF cores. When cutting veneer panels, I also like to use a zero-clearance throat plate and burnish some blue masking tape on the cut line. One more trick that can lead to crisp edges is to raise the blade to full height so that it has more of a downward cut.

ROUTER BITS

There are flush-trim router bits or pattern copying bits with bearings that can clean and flush up both solid and veneered edging. I tend not to use these for this task for two reasons. Unless the bits are extremely sharp, I find that they can damage the edging.

Various flush-trimming router bits. Those with bearings work much better.

When veneering, switch from the combination blade to a dedicated plywood/veneer blade.

The second reason is that there is usually glue squeeze-out and if the bearing hits these, you are not going to be flush. I typically use these bits to create exact duplicates from templates such as those in Chapter 6 and Chapter 10.

FILES & SCRAPERS

When it comes to working with veneer, you don't need top-of-the-line files and scrapers. Solid, reasonably priced tools will do the trick.

A file is going to be one of your most-used tools when cleaning up veneer edging. As demonstrated throughout the projects in this book, you'll use the teeth on the side of the file and, if you've glued the edging or capping properly, you should have

no tear out. Always work toward the center of your piece and not during the backstroke. It will be easier to cut the edging if you clean your files often with a file card or brush. If your file gets clogged, you can damage the veneer surface.

Using a mill file for the clean-up is ideal. If you use a fine-toothed file, it will clog more quickly, causing you to stop and clean repeatedly. A shear file can be used on harder drying glues, such as hot hide glue or even urea-based glues, like Unibond 800.

Card scrapers and cabinet scrapers can all be used in cleaning up glue, rough spots, or even solid wood edging. Always use a delicate touch and a light cut.

Scrapers will clean up glue and rough spots while files will be your most-used tool when cleaning up edging.

TOOL CHECKLIST

Sometimes it's helpful to eyeball all the tools you might eventually need listed on one page. You can check off what you have and pick up the rest as you need them.

TAPE

- Veneer tape
- Packing tape
- Green masking or binding tape
- Blue masking or painter's tape
- Tape dispenser

GLUE

- Polyvinyl acetate (PVA) adhesives
- Cyanoacrylate (CA) or "crazy glue"
- Liquid hide glue
- Hide glue
- Glue pot or wax heater
- Veneer hammer
- Thermometer
- Glue brush
- Brayer or small hand roller
- Notched plastic trowel
- Glue paddle or glue mixer

CLAMPS

- Cauls
- Three-way edge clamp
- Spindle clamp
- *F*-style clamp
- Parallel or pipe clamps
- One-handed edge clamp

CUTTING

- Veneer saw
- Utility knife
- Scalpel-style craft knife
- Self-healing craft mat
- Straightedge
- Scissors
- Veneer jointer

SANDING

- Sanding paper, 120–220 grit
- Sanding block
- Shooting sander
- Random orbit sander
- Popsicle sticks
- Tongue depressors
- Brush

FILES, SCRAPERS & PLANES

- Mill file
- Shear cut file (such as Super-Shear)
- Card scraper
- Cabinet scraper
- Block plane
- Jack or jointer plane

STORAGE & SOFTENING

- Shelving
- Heater, humidifier, or dehumidifier
- Veneer softener
- Brown paper
- Newsprint

OTHER TOOLS

- Plywood/veneer tablesaw blades
- Flush-trim and pattern copying router bits
- Roarockit kit
- VacuPress bag and pump
- Waxilit
- Clothes iron
- Veneer press screws (such as Shop Fox)

CHAPTER 5

MAGNETIC MESSAGE BOARD

Ironing: Not Just for Wrinkled Clothes Anymore

This project is an excellent way to get started. You probably have all the tools and adhesives on hand; it uses a substrate other than plywood or MDF; and it really shows how easy veneering can be. Best of all, when you're done, you'll have a handy magnetic message board in the entryway to keep you from misplacing your keys.

THE CONCEPT

We're going to make a magnetic bulletin board using a plain-old clothes iron and yellow glue. The first time I saw this technique, I was skeptical. How can this work without an expensive vacuum press or a truckload of clamps? To be honest, it feels like cheating. The idea is to coat the surfaces with glue, let them dry, and, with some heat, re-activate the glue while pressing everything together. I've found that any type of PVA glue works. If you're going to use Titebond II or III, be prepared to iron within 24 hours. With Titebond Original you can wait even weeks with no ill effect.

In this project, we'll apply the veneers over a thin piece of inexpensive 22-gauge sheet metal (available at any hardware or hobby store). For the veneer, we'll use raw commercial veneer around $\frac{1}{42}$". If you use a thicker veneer, your results start to vary at $\frac{1}{16}$" because more heat is required and that can cause cracks. Keep it simple: go with less than $\frac{1}{16}$" and use a couple of pieces that are tame, don't need to be flattened, and have a pleasing design. (My friend gave me some great quartersawn sapele veneer that's been looking for the right project; this'll be it.)

This project applies one of the rules from earlier: you'll veneer both sides. It's such a small project you can use the same veneer on the back. No need to break out a different backer veneer.

The veneered sheet is encased in a solid wood frame with a cleat for easy hanging. I used black walnut because it pairs well with the sapele. If your veneer has swirls, stay with a straight grain for the frame. The top frame piece is part of the cleat and the joinery is made up of simple butt joints reinforced with dowels or screws.

To keep the peace at home, go out and get a cheap iron with a nonstick base and a high (cotton) setting that can reach close to 400° F (204° C). Otherwise, make sure that house iron is cleaned up nice and good. (Don't say I didn't warn you.)

TOOLS & MATERIALS

- Acetone and finish of choice
- Ruler with self-adhesive sandpaper
- Blue masking tape
- Knife with sharp blade
- Newspaper or kraft paper
- Water mister
- PVA glue (such as Titebond Original)
- Brayer, glue brush, and injector
- Router table with ³⁄₁₆" straight bit
- Clothes iron
- Random-orbit sander
- Clamps

CUT LIST

QTY	PIECE	MATERIAL	L	W	T
1	Magnetic core	Ferrous sheet metal	24"	6"	22 ga.
2	Faces	Veneer	24"	6"	<¹⁄₁₆"
2	Side rails	Hardwood	23½"	¾"	⅝"
1	Top rail	Hardwood	7"	¾"	⅝"
1	Bottom shelf	Hardwood	9"	2½"	½"
1	Cleat	Hardwood	5¼"	1½"	¼"
4	Fasteners	Dowels or wood screws	12"	-	¼" dia.
	Groove fillers	Hardwood	~ 55"	¼"	⅛"

PROJECT PLANS

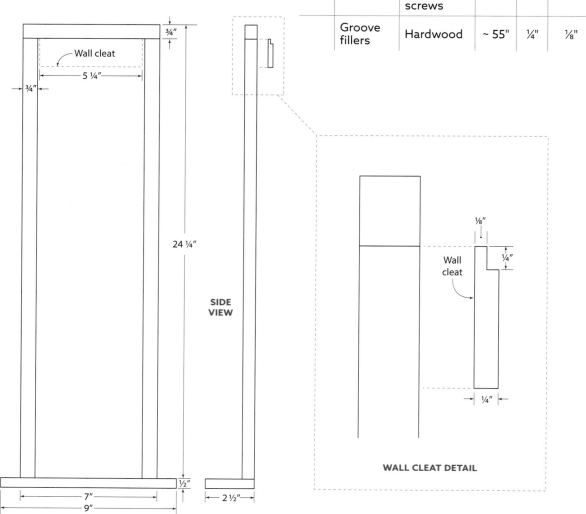

SIDE VIEW

WALL CLEAT DETAIL

PREP YOUR MATERIALS

A Gather everything you need to start your project. Make sure you purchase stainless steel and not aluminum, or the panel won't be magnetic. (Sadly, I speak from experience.) **B** Use acetone to clean the sheet metal on both sides and let it dry. **C** Use a cutting mat or sacrificial piece of wood to cut your veneer pieces 1" longer and wider than your metal piece. Use a ruler with self-adhesive sandpaper on the back and blue masking tape across the grain for straight cuts and no tearing. **D** As outlined in Chapter 4, a knife with a sharp blade is perfect for this project. **E** Remember when you're done to peel the masking tape against itself to avoid damaging the veneers.

APPLY THE GLUE

A Cover your work surface with newsprint or kraft paper to catch excess adhesive. When applying glue to one side of veneer, it tends to curl. To counteract this, mist the back with water. (Misting is the key word here, not drenching.) **B** Tape down the corners of the veneer to prevent curling before working with the glue. **C** Apply the glue. **D** Use a brayer or other spreader to evenly coat the glue to one side of each sheet of veneer and the sheet metal core. Make sure there are no puddles or dry spots by removing or adding glue as needed. Depending on shop conditions, the drying can take from a few hours to overnight with the veneer changing color and taking on a glistening sheen. For the sheet metal core, once the glue is dry to the touch flip it over and coat the second face.

MAKE THE FRAME

A While the glue dries, gather up the solid wood pieces to be milled for the frame. To keep it simple, the side rails will be doweled to the top piece and bottom shelf. This allows the side rail grooves to run full length while the top and bottom pieces will have stopped grooves. To cut the grooves, choose the equipment and method that works best for you. Simply adjust the thickness and length of each piece of the frame accordingly. **B** These grooves are cut with a ³⁄₁₆" straight bit on the router table to create grooves ³⁄₁₆" wide by ¼" deep. All pieces are referenced from the back with the groove started ¼" from the fence, leaving a pleasant reveal of ³⁄₁₆" on the face. One of the final steps includes filling the side grooves with ⅛"-thick material to pin the sheet metal core tightly towards the front. Set the pieces aside until you're ready to assemble the frame.

PRESS THE VENEERS

A When the glue on both the veneer and sheet metal are dry to the touch, it's time to press the veneers. Plug in the iron and set it to the hottest temperature. Make sure it's empty of water because you don't want to introduce any steam; water-based adhesives cure when water is evaporated. **B** Place kraft paper on your bench and lay down the first veneer sheet with the glued surface facing up. Next place the sheet metal core on top with an even reveal all around, and then sandwich it with the second veneer sheet, glue side down.

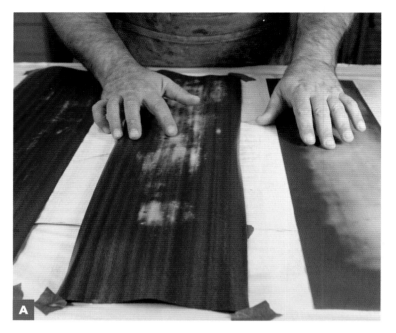

C Make a test run of your iron on the veneer. If it has a nonstick base and slides easily, it's perfectly acceptable to use it right on the veneer. **D** If it doesn't, place kraft paper between the iron and the veneer. To be safe, use the kraft paper regardless of the iron to reduce the chance of burning the veneer. When ironing, press down firmly and move in a smooth and steady motion from one side to the other. Don't move the iron back and forth rapidly. While it's usually best to start from the center and move outwards, this piece is small enough to work in one direction. Feel for any bubbles and press them out if needed. The sheet metal will transfer heat to the other side, so it should require only a light pass on the back to tack it in place. Let it cool to allow the glue to fully cure and harden. **NOTE** Don't be tempted to fiddle with the overhang of veneer too soon. It will result in bad edges around the sheet metal core. (Again, I sadly speak from experience...)

TRIM THE VENEER

A Use a sharp breakaway blade knife to trim the excess veneer from the sides. Don't try to trim to the edge of the metal core from top to bottom in one pass. Go slowly and use shallow cuts on the sides until you feel the metal core. **B** To trim the ends, place your ruler at the points where the core ends, which should now be visible via the side, and trim with multiple passes from each surface. **C** Don't worry if you get some cracks in the veneer while trimming. **D** You can simply reheat the veneer and make a seamless repair. **NOTE** If you have a jagged edge of veneer that reveals some of the metal core around the edges, no worries; the groove will hide any inconsistencies.

A

SAND, DRY-ASSEMBLE & DRILL HOLES

A For the frame pieces, use a handplane, sander, or whatever works best, but the veneer core will need to be sanded as handplaning commercial veneer will not work. A random-orbit sander works best, but hand sanding is also acceptable. If you handled the veneer carefully, you won't need more than 180 grit. If you want to go higher, don't surpass 220 grit. Remember, it's thin; there's only so much veneer to sand! **B** Once all the pieces are clean and smooth, use two clamps to bring everything together for a dry fit. Level the back of all the frame pieces and make sure you have equal distances between the two side rails at the top and bottom. Then, using either a drill press or a handheld drill or driver, mark and drill ¼" holes that are 1½" deep for the dowels. Be aware of the grooves on the side rails to avoid drilling into them and hitting the core. If you'd rather not use dowels, countersunk wood screws and plugs will also work.

B

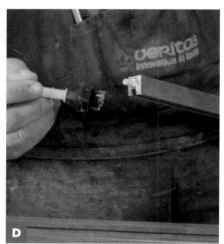

GLUE IT UP

A After the dry assembly, you know everything fits and your dowel holes in the top and bottom are aligned with the side rails. It's time to put it all together. Prep your glue so you can dab it with a glue brush. **B** Apply glue to the dowel holes in the rails. **C** Insert the dowels. **D** Brush the exposed dowels with more glue. **E** Clamp everything up to let the adhesive cure completely.

A

INSERT GROOVE FILLER & CLEAT

A With the assembled project still in the clamps, flip it over carefully and inject a bead of glue into the gap between the core and the rail.
B Gently insert the groove filler pieces into the sides and bottom.
C The groove at the top will be filled using a cleat style of hanger.
D Create the rabbet for the cleat and make sure it fits snugly into the top groove before it's installed on to the wall for hanging.

B

C

D

FINISHING TOUCHES

A When the glue has dried, flush all joints with your preferred method and touch up any scuff marks from the clamping process. Any finish will work for this piece including just wax, shellac, polyurethane, or even a Danish oil.

Locate the spot to hang your board and screw the rabbeted cleat into the wall. Level it and mount your newly minted magnetic message board. Mine hangs right by the front door. It not only holds notes, reminders, and the occasional receipt, but also my keys. **B** While any magnet will do the trick, rare earth magnets will give you that extra holding power and can be bought with either a knob or a hook. And, if you're feeling really creative, you can always attach magnets to small rocks or found objects to make your own custom fixture.

WRAPPING UP

Wasn't that easy? The frame portion took up most of your time, tools, and brain power. The veneer portion—not so much—which is a good thing because you got to handle veneer, glue, and an iron without venturing into anything too complicated.

Plus, the dimensions of the project make it easy to find veneer wide enough without having to join two or more pieces. If you're feeling comfortable, it's very easy to make this piece larger using the techniques and the jointing jig in Chapter 4.

DO'S & DON'TS OF RANDOM-ORBIT SANDING

1 Don't linger in one spot. Use a steady and smooth action across the workpiece.

2 Keep the sander on the workpiece when approaching the edges. (Get a harder pad for flat surfaces, if possible.)

3 Don't force the sander down. It wants to sand; just let it do its job.

4 Use a connected vacuum for best results. Dust bags collect some dust, but a vacuum is best for your health and work. When the edging is a different species than your veneer, a vacuum prevents edge dust from impregnating the veneer. Remember to reduce the suction when working on final passes and finer grits.

5 Don't tilt the sander in an attempt to get at a spot; try to feather it out.

6 No need to use every grit in succession, but don't jump too far from one grit to the next. If you're careful handling the veneer, start at 150 grit or even 180 grit and finish up at 220 grit. With a clean, scratch-free surface, it's fine to stop at 220 grit.

7 Don't use worn-out sanding discs. Replace them when they no longer cut.

8 REMEMBER: WE ONLY HAVE SO MUCH VENEER TO SAND!

NOTE If you decide to buy a new sander for veneering, look for a model with a small sanding stroke, such as ⅛". You don't need the sander or the sanding disks to be too aggressive. Most of today's sanders come with a speed setting and I typically adjust mine to a medium level. Keep it slow to make sure you're in control and it doesn't wobble all over.

CHAPTER 6

THE FLOATING TOP SIDE TABLE

Hammer Veneering: But You Don't Actually Hammer It

The term "hammer veneering" seems a little deceiving. There is a bit of tapping involved, but the bulk of the process is more like using a hard squeegee to push around hot and sticky syrup instead of water.

THE CONCEPT

This side table is an excellent project for learning how to use both hot hide glue and liquid hide glue. And, because you can never have enough side tables, it will be a useful—and stylish—addition in whatever room you decide to place it. The table is designed so that it appears to have a floating top while the shaped aprons will give it a different look when viewed from different angles.

Hot hide glue has been used by many woodworkers for a very, very long time. How long, you ask? Like, *discovered-intact-on-furniture-found-in-Egyptian-tombs* kind of long. And it's ideal for veneering because it's very forgiving. Hot hide glue can be worked again and again or reversed by simply heating it up and adding moisture. The drawback is it can get a little sticky and messy, so make sure you cover your work surfaces with newsprint or brown kraft paper. You might also want to have some rags and vinegar ready to clean up your hands, the hammer, and any other tools. (Yup, vinegar...)

One key benefit of this project is learning the value of a good mock-up versus a sketch or drawing (see the sidebar on page 89), which allows you to see your design at full size. Since the table is not square, it needs the aprons to have similar profiles, but different lengths. The two templates you make will be used to shape the veneered aprons. So spend as much time as needed to make the templates because any imperfections will be duplicated onto the apron pieces. (But, don't stress about it too much; imperfections only make your finished piece more original.)

TOOLS & MATERIALS

- Knife with sharp blade; straightedge
- Blue masking, veneer, and double-sided tapes
- Sanding shooter
- Glue pot, hide glue, Old Brown hide glue, jar, and brush
- Titebond Liquid Hide Glue

- Veneer hammer
- Heat gun or iron
- File and brush
- Tablesaw with crosscut sled
- French curve and plywood apron template
- Bandsaw
- Router with flush-trim bit

- Spindle sander and random-orbit sander
- Clamps and cauls
- Drill
- Finish of choice

PROJECT PLANS

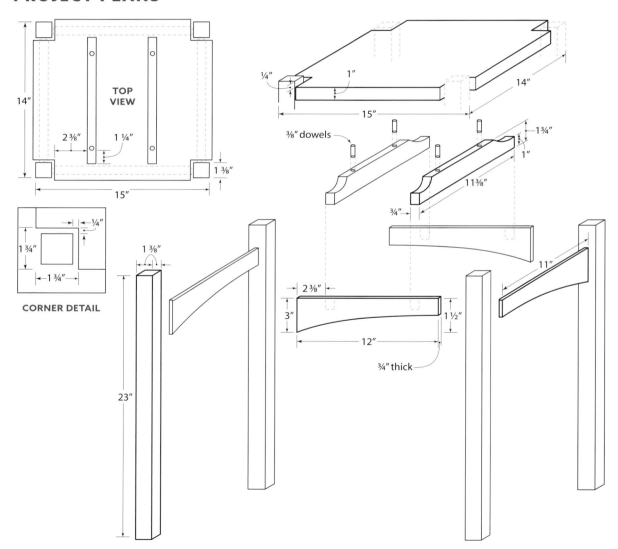

CUT LIST

QTY	PIECE	MATERIAL	L	W	T
2 (2)	Tabletop core (and faces)	MDF (Imbuia burl veneer)	15"	14"	½" (<¹⁄₁₆")
2 (4)	Apron cores (and faces), short	MDF (Imbuia burl veneer)	11"	1½" –3"	¾" (<¹⁄₁₆")
2 (4)	Apron cores (and faces), long	MDF (Imbuia burl veneer)	12"	1½" –3"	¾" (<¹⁄₁₆")
2 (2)	Tabletop edges, long (and short)	Imbuia burl veneer	11½" (10½")	1"	<¹⁄₁₆"
8	Tabletop corner edges	Imbuia burl veneer	1¾"	1"	<¹⁄₁₆"
4	Long aprons, top and bottom edges	Imbuia burl veneer	12" and 12³⁄₁₆"	¾"	<¹⁄₁₆"
4	Short aprons, top and bottom edges	Imbuia burl veneer	11" and 11³⁄₁₆"	¾"	<¹⁄₁₆"
8	Apron edges	Imbuia burl veneer	1½" and 3"	¾"	<¹⁄₁₆"
4	Legs	Solid walnut	23"	1³⁄₈"	1³⁄₈"
2	Floating supports	Solid walnut	11³⁄₈"	1¾"	¾"

*If there are two parts that differ only by one measurement, such as a substrate and its veneer face (thickness, in this case), both are shown in one line with the differences in parentheses. Other columns in that line without a parenthetical option are the same for both parts.

PREPARE THE TABLETOP

Glue up two pieces of ½" MDF about 1" to 1½" wider and longer than the final size of the table. This will give you plenty of real estate to clean up the edges. **A** Cut the veneer. If you need to join two pieces then use the techniques outlined in Chapter 4 and the following steps. **B** For this project, I was having trouble handplaning the edges clean, so I used a couple of MDF boards to hold down the veneer while I jointed their edges with a sanding shooter. When it comes to burl veneers, sanding the edge is sometimes the only option. (And later, when you add the hot hide glue to the veneers, it will act as a softener and it can be worked very nicely.)

(continued on next page)

A

B

PREPARE THE TABLETOP
(continued)

C Once you have clean and crisp edges, apply masking tape to the glue side and number each piece and the edges to be joined. **D** Line up the seams to be joined. **E** Apply masking tape to hold them together temporarily. **F** Apply the veneer tape to the face side. Repeat steps C through F for the opposite face. **G** Sandwich both joined veneer sheets between MDF boards with a weight on top while the tape dries.

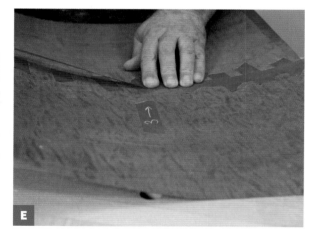

GETTING THE HIDE GLUE READY

Plug in and turn on the wax heater or glue pot. Add water to the bowl and heat it to 150° F (65° C). **A** Place the working edge of the hammer on the body of the heater so it's warm when working the veneer. In the meantime, add some hide glue granules to a glass jar and cover it with cold water. **B** Let it sit until the mixture looks like lumpy oatmeal. This should take anywhere from 30 minutes to an hour. When the water has been absorbed by the glue, place the jar in your heat pot and let that melt to the consistency of runny syrup. You want it to run off the brush in a steady stream rather than droplets or beads. If it gets too thick, add more water. If it's too thin, take the lid off the jar and let the water evaporate until you get the right consistency. Replace the lid to stop the evaporation. **C** As the glue is prepping, try to keep the shop warm—along with the substrate and veneers—to extend the time you have to work with it. If needed, you can heat up the surfaces with a heat gun or clothes iron and work it some more.

NOTE Before tackling a large project, practice using hide glue on small scraps of plywood or MDF and cutoffs from veneer pieces. To see if you have the correct consistency, "mop" the glue over the substrate and go over some of the areas with glue on it already. If it lumps up or builds up, it is too thick, and you should add a bit of water to the jar. In most circumstances, you'll want to add water.

NOTE Traditionally, substrate surfaces were roughed up prior to hide gluing, usually with a toothing plane. However, I often skip this step (even with MDF) and everything turns out fine. Try a test for yourself—if the pieces are still glued together the next morning, you're good to go.

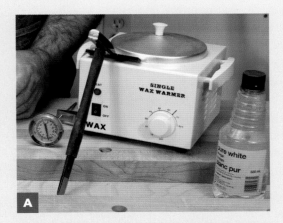

A

B

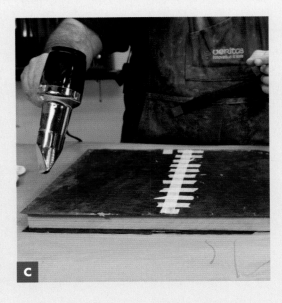

C

APPLY THE GLUE

When the glue is ready for application, remove the masking tape from the glue side of the veneer. Be ready to work fast; the glue will get cold and start to tack up quickly.  **A** Using your newly made brush from Chapter 3 (page 35) (or a purchased one), apply the glue liberally to the MDF core. **B** Lay the veneer show-face down on the MDF. This may seem strange, but will help keep the glue warm. Also, the bit of glue that transfers

to the show side will serve as a slide aid for the hammer. **C** Apply more hide glue to the exposed surface. **D** Peel the veneer off the substrate and lay it show-face up this time. **E** Use your veneer hammer to start pushing the veneer into the substrate from the center out. Add more glue to the top if needed. This will also serve to heat some of the glue underneath, allowing you more time to work. Any glue that you squeeze out can be added back into the glass jar and will melt and be reusable. **F** If you find that you can't get around to the whole surface, work in sections by using a heat gun or iron to heat up a section then work it over with the hammer. Look for areas that did not get pressed flat. Try heating those areas up along with the surrounding area and try again to work the bubbles out.

Repeat the steps for the opposite face and then let the tabletop fully cure overnight or even longer. Remember to prop the panel up rather than laying it flat on the workbench to prevent warping.

CLEANING UP THE EDGES

A Once fully cured, clean one edge of the panel using a file. Normally, a mill file will do the job, however, hot hide glue dries very hard and a shear cut file might be a better option. **B** Clean the file often, as it will get jammed with dried glue and veneer. **C** Joint that edge. **D** Using a crosscut sled on the tablesaw, trim the ends and rip the final edge. **NOTE** While it's OK to clean up the edges, leave the top oversize for now because the base has to be assembled before arriving at the final dimensions of the tabletop.

DOUBLE-CHECK THE GLUE

If you notice any areas that didn't get glued down or that bubbled up, it's time to work on those areas. **A** Using an iron, heat up the areas in question. **B** Use a scraper or hammer to press the veneer down. **C** If there is a raised area that won't stay down, first heat it with the iron. **D** Create a small slit with a sharp knife and either place more glue inside or remove glue if there is too much.

NOTE Running your nails across the surface and listening for change in tone or tapping the surface can alert you to problem areas.

CLEAN UP THE PANEL SURFACES

It's time to clean up the excess hide glue and veneer tape on the surface of the panels. No need to be extremely thorough at this point as you'll complete a final sanding before applying a finish. **A** Dampen a clean rag with hot water and rub over the veneer surface. **B** Gently remove the veneer tape. **C** For stubborn spots, a scraper will do the trick. **D** Sandpaper also comes in handy for any hard-to-remove glue and tape.

PREPARING THE APRONS

Using the same steps to veneer, cure, and clean up the tabletop, repeat the process for the aprons. You'll veneer two sides of one larger panel of ¾" MDF. To create a curved bottom template, use a French curve to draw a pleasing shape on two different pieces of plywood (the short and long aprons; see illustration). Cut out the templates with the bandsaw.

CUT THE APRONS

A Using double-sided tape, attach the templates you created to the apron panel. **B** Cut out the aprons close to the template on the bandsaw. Leave at least ⅛" of material around the template. Take care not to accidentally cut into the template. **C** Shape the aprons using a flush-trim bit on the router table. Repeat this process for the second pair of aprons.

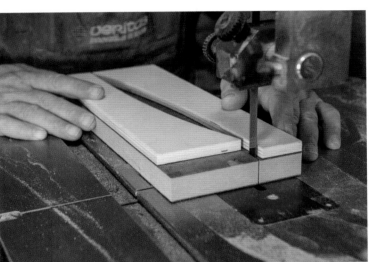

MILL THE LEGS & FLOATING SUPPORTS

A Mill up the stock for the legs and floating supports. Use rift-sawn areas of a plank for the legs and this should give you straight lines up and down their length. The floating supports are made of solid walnut and have curves cut on the tops to further hide them from view. Use French curves to draw the curve. Then, cut them out on the bandsaw and smooth them with a spindle sander.

DRY-FIT THE APRONS

B Use the cabinetmaker's triangle on both the legs and the aprons and arrange them for joinery. **NOTE** You can use any method you choose, from pocket screws and dowels to Festool's DOMINO connectors. **C** Complete a dry fit with clamps to determine the final dimensions of the tabletop.

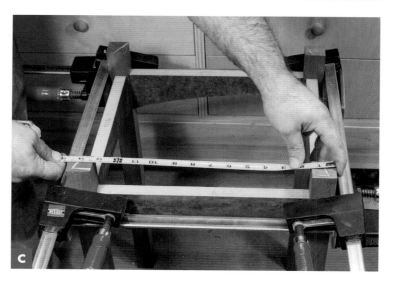

CUT THE TABLETOP

A To set up for the corner cutouts, use a stop block on the crosscut sled to get an even square. Double-check this measurement on scrap pieces and, once determined, lock the height of the blade. Place blue masking tape on the areas to be cut and burnish them in. Complete the eight cuts on the corners.

BEGIN TO APPLY EDGING TO THE TOP

The same veneer for the tabletop and aprons will hide the MDF core. Cut veneer that is wider and longer than the corners of the tabletop. **B** Start up the wax warmer and add a bottle of Old Brown hide glue. Heat it to about 140° F (60° C). **C** We will work in pairs (see Photo D). Apply the heated glue to both surfaces. **D** Attach the veneer using a clamp and caul. Repeat steps for the edge pair on the other side of the tabletop. **NOTE** Hide glue will stick to masking tape; be as clean as you can.

EDGE THE APRON

As the first two tabletop corners cure, focus on the aprons. Cut veneer pieces a little wider and longer than the apron. **A** Apply Old Brown hide glue to the apron. **B** Apply glue to the veneer. **C** Clamp the aprons with cauls and let them cure. For the curved bottoms, use three pieces of 1/8" hardboard for the caul. It will follow the contour and apply pressure while the glue does its job.

CONTINUE THE EDGING

D When the glue has fully cured on the first two pairs of corner edging veneers, trim up the overhanging portions of veneer. As long as you put enough glue on the edges, you will get a clean cut. **E** Clean it up further with the teeth on the side of a mill file. Make sure you have about three wraps of masking tape on the end of the file so that it does not scratch the veneered tabletop surface. Trim and flush the previously glued edges before gluing and clamping new edging. Glue on some more edging to the mating corners of the top and repeat the steps as above two more times, covering up all exposed MDF edges.

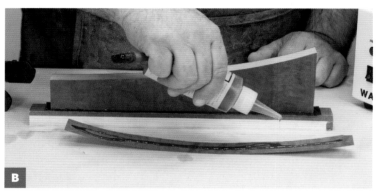

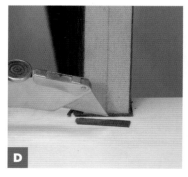

BLEND THE SURFACES

A Using a smooth file and/or sandpaper, work the two edges together, sanding at a 45°-angle from each edge. **B** Use a light touch; in short order, two or three passes, any seam will almost disappear.

SMOOTH IT OUT

Use a random-orbit sander on the top and aprons. Start at 150 or 180 grit. Don't linger too long in any one spot; remember, you only have so much veneer to work with. Use the power sander to complete a general cleaning. **C** Any small rough spots can be dealt with by hand-sanding with a block or even loose sandpaper. No need to go higher than 220 grit; if 180 gives you a nice surface, feel free to stop there. Don't forget to either plane or sand the legs and floating supports as well.

REPAIR TIP FOR CHIPS AND NICKS

One of the apron's edges got chipped during the clean-up process. **A** To repair it, I tested different colors of stain markers on a scrap piece of MDF to determine the best match.

B Then I applied brown-tinted medium cyano-acrylate glue to fill the gap. **C** A quick shot of accelerator hardened the glue instantly. A little sanding completed a near-invisible repair.

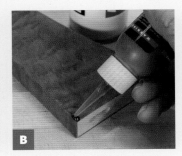

PUT IT TOGETHER

For this project, I used Festool Dominoes. But, as mentioned earlier, complete using the joinery you are comfortable with. **A** After the holes are bored, use liquid hide glue to attach the pieces in sections. Attach a pair of legs to the corresponding shorter aprons, then repeat the process for the other pair of legs. When the glue cures and sets, join those assemblies to each other with the second set of aprons and the floating supports. Use as many clamps and cauls as you needed during the practice run.

CONNECT THE TABLETOP

B Once the base is fully cured, use masking tape to measure and mark dowel placement for connecting the tabletop to the base. Check your measurements as many times as you need to feel comfortable that they are correct. **C** Use an awl and a brad-point bit to drill to

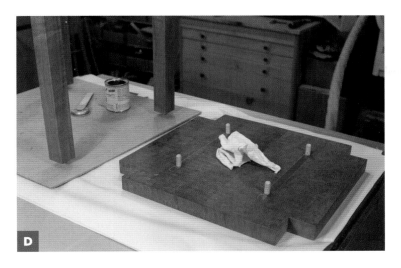

the appropriate depths, first in the supports and then the tabletop.

 While you could do this on the drill press, doing them by hand as accurately as possible works fine, maybe even better. The slight errors that creep in with hand drilling actually create a bit of tension that holds the two parts together better.

Before finally gluing the tabletop to the base, do any final touchups and then apply a finish.

WRAPPING UP

Hopefully, this table will last you a few lifetimes. However, if it should get damaged, you'll be able to apply a couple of key lessons and tricks learned in this project. You can reverse the hide glue with some heat and warm water and apply a new piece of veneer for a perfect repair. Or you can use a stain marker and some tinted glue to smooth out any nicks and dings.

IN PRAISE OF THE MOCKUP

For this side table, I chose to make an actual-size mockup to visualize what I had in mind. Mockups are much better than sketches when you're unsure about some of the details in a project. They can be ripped apart and joined back together with hot glue, brads, and screws. The exercise proved helpful. In the end, I didn't like the shaped legs (shown here) or the tapered legs (not shown) that I originally designed, so I stuck with 1⅜" square legs that extend ¼" higher than the top.

CHAPTER 7

VENEER PRESS

Dedicated Setup: Take the Chore Out of Pressing

There are lots of ways to mechanically press veneers. I've laid a few bricks or even gym weights on top of a veneer sandwich while the glue cures. However, building a dedicated and simple press ends the task of gathering clamps and making cambered cauls and stand-offs. It takes the chore out of pressing when the setup is right there whenever you want to veneer.

THE CONCEPT

We are going to build a medium-sized veneer pressing station with screws that are available online or at your woodworking supplier. The screws range from inexpensive on up. For this project, I've used six screws made by Shop Fox. However, expanding this setup to include more is very easy. For small pressings, I've built a version with just one screw and another press containing a pair of them.

Over the years, I've seen different variations of veneer presses that, instead of screws, use small bottle-style car jacks, or even an actual book press for small panels. You can also use regular woodworking *F*-style clamps and cambered cauls, but I find that creating and using this project is less of a chore. If you search for "veneer press" online, you'll see different versions, with sizes ranging from one screw to others large enough to complete a dining room table.

Once the press is built, we'll use it to make the project in Chapter 8: a tea tray along with a little box to house a pair of cups and some tea or other accessories. It will be the perfect project to test out your new press.

While I prefer my furniture to have a look and a feel that leans to the light and delicate, my shop fixtures and jigs are the exact opposite. I usually build them like tanks and this veneer press is no exception. We'll use three pieces of ¾" MDF to construct a solid base that can be firmly pressed against. Hard maple will be used as the frame members because the more screws that are added, the sturdier a frame is required. Ideally, if you want to expand this to a much larger size, the best way to do it would be a torsion box as a base. In the spirit of not overthinking too far down the road, for now you shouldn't have any issues using this veneer press as shown.

TOOLS & MATERIALS

- Tablesaw with crosscut sled
- Clamps
- Drill with 1 1/4" Forstner, countersink, and pilot bits for #8 screws
- (18) #8 x 1 1/4" flat-head screws
- Sandpaper or chisel
- Glue
- Straightedge
- (6) press clamps, such as Shop Fox D2893
- (12) #8 x 1" round-head screws
- Hard paste wax

CUT LIST

QTY	PIECE	MATERIAL	L	W	T
3	Base	MDF	30"	18"	¾"
6	Legs	Dense hardwood	14"	2¼"	1¾"
3	Stretchers	Dense hardwood	18"	2¼"	1¾"

*If there are two parts that differ only by one measurement, such as a substrate and its veneer face (thickness, in this case), both are shown in one line with the differences in parentheses. Other columns in that line without a parenthetical option are the same for both parts.

PROJECT PLANS / MEASURED ILLUSTRATION

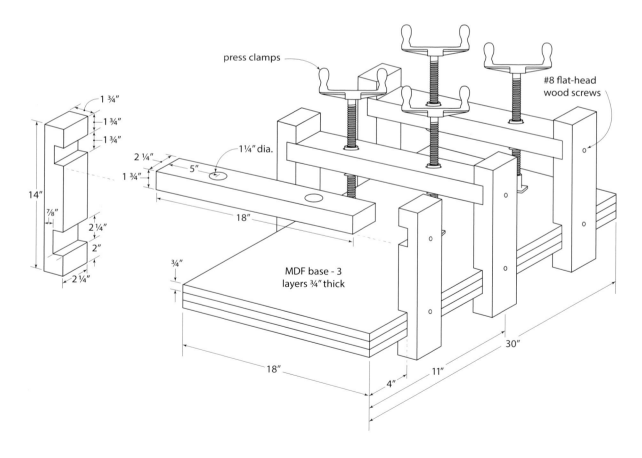

press clamps

#8 flat-head wood screws

1 ¾"
1 ¾"
1 ¾"
14"
7⁄8"
2 ¼"
2"
2 ¼"

2 ¼"
5"
1 ¾"
1¼" dia.
18"

MDF base - 3 layers ¾" thick

¾"
18"
4"
11"
30"

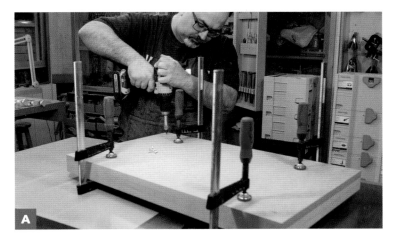

CUT & PREP THE BASE

By starting with the base, you can turn your attention to the frame pieces while the glue cures. **A** Cut your three MDF pieces to the specified length and width. Using a few clamps, stack and dry fit the three pieces together, making sure that all the edges are flush. **B** In the corners, roughly 1" in from the edges, pilot drill and countersink holes from both of the outside faces to the center core for the #8 x 1¼" screws. Next, mark the cabinetmaker's triangle on one edge across all three pieces so it can be reassembled in the same orientation. **C** Loosen the clamps and, using either sandpaper or a chisel, smooth the areas around the freshly drilled holes. Drilling MDF always leaves raised edges on holes unless a sharp new bit is used.

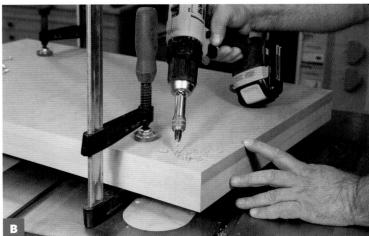

GLUE THE BASE

A Spread some glue on one of the faces of the center piece. **B** Paying attention to the cabinetmaker's triangle, place the corresponding outer piece on top. **C** Start screwing the two pieces together and you'll find that the two pieces will slip a little as the screw finds its mark. By the time you drive the second screw in, you'll have nice and flush edges. Drive in the remaining pair of screws, then turn the assembly over and repeat the steps of applying glue and screwing.

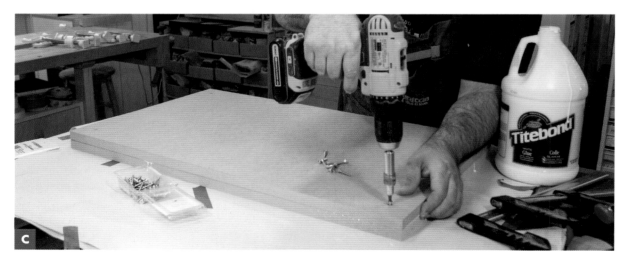

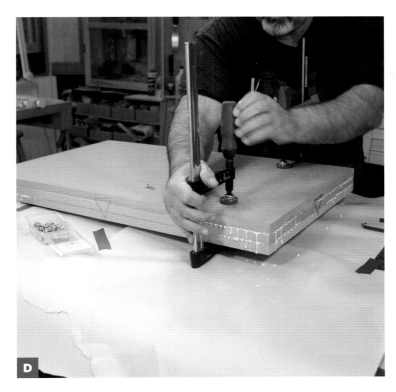

D We'll use some clamps to help add pressure to the assembly. A few deep-reaching *F*-style clamps will get pressure toward the middle, while others will do their magic on the perimeter. **E** Using a straightedge, check that the base is remaining flat and free of any minor humps or valleys. Unless there are puddles of glue, there shouldn't be too much trouble ensuring flatness. MDF is great for establishing smoothness and flatness. If needed, you can add three or four more screws to the center of both the top and bottom and a few near the perimeter to level out the base. **NOTE** Don't use wet rags to clean up the squeeze-out; MDF and water do not get along.

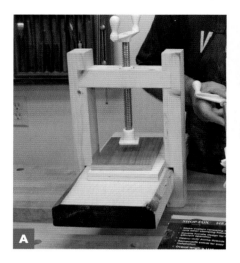

MAKE THE FRAME PIECES

Turning our attention to the frame pieces, mill up some hard maple. If you don't have hard maple, ash or any dense hardwood will work. Just stay away from lumber that has any defects because the pieces will be under a lot of pressure when in use. On this single-screw version made for my shop, 2 x 4s can be used, but hardwoods are preferred, especially when adding more press screws.  Create the dados at the top and bottom of the legs using a tablesaw and a crosscut sled. While this is probably the fastest and more accurate method, this step can also be done with a combination of power tools and hand tools, on a router table, or on a bandsaw. And, if you have a dado set, that will speed it along even more.  Both sets of dados are ⅞" deep, halfway into the thickness of the legs. The length of the dados on the bottom is 2¼", which is the thickness of MDF base, and 1¾" at the top, which accounts for the horizontal stretcher containing the press clamps.

SCREW SPACING ON A VENEER PRESS

Let's talk a little about the spacing of the screws. One of my instructors had a veneer press with screws spaced up to 7½" apart. I'm more comfortable with a 6" space around each pad of the screw, which means that I don't space the next clamp more than 12" from the first. In fact, since we don't glue the frame members to either the base or the stretcher, we can move one frame assembly closer or farther from the nearest set according to the needs of the project. The wood screws that are added serve only as locating pins.

ASSEMBLE THE FRAMING STRETCHERS

A Using a 1¼" Forstner bit, drill a pair of holes evenly spaced through the stretchers. To do this, mark the middle of the stretcher and then split each section into two and you will have found the locations of these holes. The pair of holes are for the bushings on the press screws. While this hole is not a perfect, snug fit, it doesn't have to be. The ideal bore is 1³⁄₁₆", but there is no need to buy a special bit for this. There are also two slots in the bushing for wood screws that will act as counter-rotation pins; however, the genius of the setup is that everything tightens up as you apply clamping pressure against the base. Even if your dados are a little loose, they will tighten up under load. **B** Use a pair of #8 x 1" round-head wood screws to secure the bushing to the stretcher. **C** Thread the press screw through the bushing. **D** Re-attach the pressure pad to complete this part of the assembly.

ASSEMBLE THE VENEER PRESS

A When the glue has cured on the base, scrape off any excess and sand any sharp edges. **B** If you have it, apply a coat of glue-resisting wax to the surface. It will greatly aid in the cleaning up of adhesives after future pressing jobs. **C** Assemble the press using #8 x 1¼" flat-head wood screws countersunk and driven through the leg and into the base. Evenly space the legs across each side of the base, making sure the opposite one lines up with the near side. **D** Seat the stretchers in their respective dados and lock their position with the same fasteners. **NOTE** Use a proper-sized pilot bit; maple and other hardwoods have a nasty habit of breaking off the heads of screws.

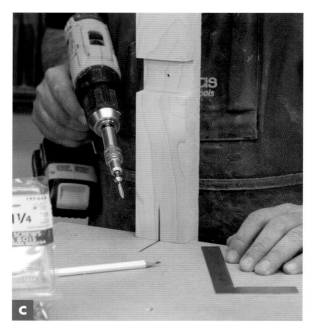

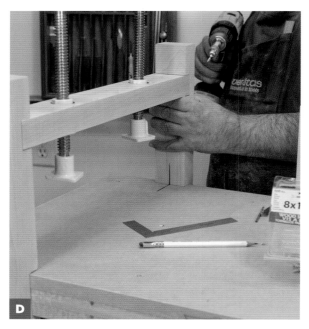

YOUR NEW VENEER PRESS IS READY TO USE

A You'll inaugurate your veneer press in Chapter 8 by gluing two pieces of ½" MDF together to create the 1"-thick core of the Tea Tray. When using the press, tighten the screws evenly, going back and forth between all of them. Listen for any cracks and creaks as you do, since this may point to an internal defect in the wood that may not have been obvious when assembling. You will also notice the stretchers flex, but the swivel action of the pressure pad will still put pressure where needed. If you're going to make a wider press and add clamps to the stretchers, make sure to use thicker and wider pieces, because you don't want them to snap. For the setup here, the listed dimensions will work fine.

A

WRAPPING UP

This press can be used for everything from small pressings to projects of medium size. Since the frame pieces are not glued to the base, they can be moved closer or further away from each other to suit the job at hand. Best of all, you can throw away the bricks, weights, and anything else you might have been using to press your veneers.

CHAPTER 8

TEA BOX & TRAY

Get Edgy: Learn to Apply Solid Edging

A few years ago, I bought a piece of live edge walnut from my local wood specialty store and the shape has grown on me. I've been toying with an idea for a nice tray or a floor lamp following the contours of that piece. In the end, like all the projects in this book, you can size and shape this tray to suit your taste and needs because the process will basically be the same. You can even skip the box and just make the tray. Same goes for the box—make one drawer, two drawers, or none.

THE CONCEPT

This project combines a few veneering concepts. First, you'll be using your new, dedicated veneer press—no more gathering clamps and making cambered cauls.

Second, you'll learn the method for applying solid-edge capping before laying on the veneer. In this project, you can have as big an overhang of veneer as is practically possible so that you can trim back to the edging caps. (You'll see with vacuum veneering in Chapters 9 and 10 that having a large overhang is not possible.)

Finally, to give the tray some substance, we'll laminate two pieces of ½" MDF. By using MDF, we don't have to put a veneer separator between the two core pieces like we have to do for the

Curved Wall Panel in Chapter 10. In fact, one of the the best pieces of design advice I've received from an instructor was to never to use standard thicknesses such as ½", ¾", or even 1" because mass-produced furniture almost always has these dimensions for its components and our eyes get acquainted to those measurements. By adding two layers of veneer to our 1" MDF core, the tray will be approximately 1³⁄₃₂" thick—a visually pleasing weight.

NOTE Once you get the hang of all the steps, you can start filling in your down time on one section by starting work on another. To keep things simple, though, I've shown you here how to create the box and tray separately.

TOOLS & MATERIALS

- Tablesaw with miter guide
- Clamps and cauls with packing tape
- Polyvinyl acetate glue, such as Titebond Cold Press for Veneer
- Jointer
- Bandsaw
- Sander of choice
- Backsaw
- Block plane

- Blue masking, veneer, and binding tape
- Knife with sharp blade
- Hammer
- Brayer
- Mill file
- Router table with bearing bit
- Small square and chisel
- Dowel centers and dowels

*If there are two parts that differ only by one measurement, such as a substrate and its veneer face (thickness, in this case), both are shown in one line with the differences in parentheses. Other columns in that line without a parenthetical option are the same for both parts.

PROJECT PLANS

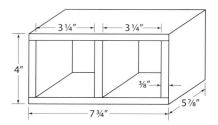

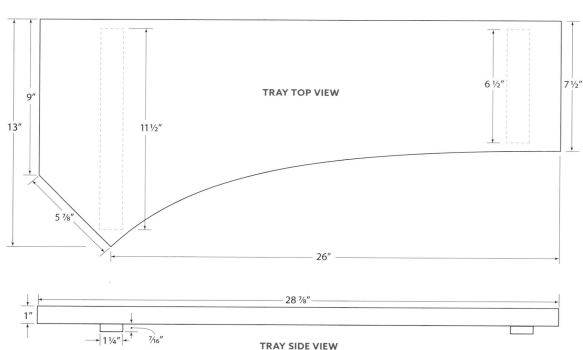

CUT LIST

QTY	PIECE	MATERIAL	L	W	T
2 (2)	Tray core (and faces)	MDF (Curly white ash veneer)	28⅞"	13" –7½"	½" (<¹⁄₁₆")
1 (1)	Tray edge, top (and bottom)	White ash	28⅞" (26")	1¼"	⅛"
1 ea.	Tray side edges	White ash	9", 5⅞", and 7½"	1¼"	⅛"
2 (4)	Box top and bottom cores (and faces)	Baltic birch plywood (Figured black limba veneer)	7¾"	5⅞"	⅜" (<¹⁄₁₆")
2 (4)	Box side cores (and faces)	Baltic birch plywood (Figured black limba veneer)	5⅞"	4"	⅜" (<¹⁄₁₆")
1 (2)	Box divider core (and faces)	Baltic birch plywood (Figured black limba veneer)	5⁷⁄₁₆"	3⁵⁄₁₆"	¼" (<¹⁄₁₆")
4	Box top and bottom, long edging	Figured black limba veneer	7¾"	⁷⁄₁₆"	<¹⁄₁₆"
4 (4)	Box sides edging, short (and long)	Figured black limba veneer	4" (5⅞")	⁷⁄₁₆"	<¹⁄₁₆"
1	Box divider edging	Figured black limba veneer	3¹⁄₁₆"	¼"	<¹⁄₁₆"
1 (2)	Back core (and faces)	Baltic birch plywood (Figured black limba veneer)	7³⁄₁₆"	3½"	¼" (<¹⁄₁₆")
1 (1)	Tray foot, short (and long)	White ash	6½" (11½")	1¼"	⁷⁄₁₆"

MAKE THE MDF CORE

Start by cutting the tray's MDF core to size and also the ¾" MDF and ⅛" hard board to be used as cauls.

A

(Make the cauls almost the full size of the press so you can reuse them.) Apply glue-resisting packing tape to the hardboard so they don't become part of the veneer sandwich.

Place one of the ¾" and ⅛" cauls on the base of the press with the taped side up. Spread glue on one face of the ½" core and lay the other piece on top. If you have a 23-gauge pin nailer, drive a few pins into the corners to keep things flush as you apply pressure. You can also use a few grains of sand to stop the slipping. **A** Place the assembly into the press, add the top cauls, and start tightening the clamps evenly. Confirm this visually with squeeze-out around the perimeter.

SHAPE THE MDF CORE

When the glue has cured, remove the core from the press. Scrape the glue off one long edge, then run it through the jointer. Using a cross-cut sled, place the freshly jointed edge against the fence and cut the core to length, slicing a bit off each end. No need to rip the last edge clean, as it will be cut off when adding our tray profile. You can shape the tray any way you want or follow this project's design. **A** Using a piece of molding, create a curve that is similar to the live edge plank. The shape is 7½" at its narrowest and 13" wide at the peak of the curve. **B** Trace the curve. Cut this out on the bandsaw and sand the edge smooth. Don't toss the cut-off; it can be used to help clamp the edge banding. Finally, cut the angled piece at the top using a miter guide on the tablesaw.

EDGE THREE SIDES OF THE CORE

A We are going to apply solid wood edging before we veneer. As the curve will be the front of the tray, we will leave that for last to hide the end grain of the side edging. **B** Using ⅛"-thick and 1 ¼"-wide white ash, glue pieces onto the edge that are a little longer than required and use masking tape–covered pine cauls and clamps. **C** After an hour or so, remove the clamps. Trim the edging close to the core with a saw. **D** A block plane or cabinet scraper makes the surface perfectly flush.

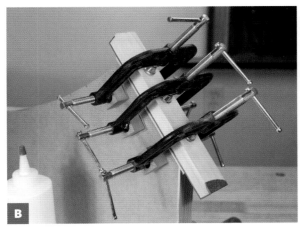

EDGE THREE SIDES OF THE CORE *(continued)*

E Continue to add edging after each previous edge is trimmed and flushed, eventually covering up the two sides and back of the tray, leaving the curved front for last.

F As detailed in Chapter 2, make sure to put masking tape on the corner of the block plane when flushing to prevent scratching.

G Pay attention to the grain direction and the sharpness of the blade. The sharper, the better. Finish off with a light sanding.

APPLY THE CURVED EDGING TO THE FRONT

A For the curved edging, use three or four pieces of ⅛"-thick hardboard that will easily bend along with the white ash edging. To resist the glue, make sure to add either masking tape or packing tape to the first piece that contacts the edging. Do a dry run or rehearsal to see how it all comes together. Look for any spots that might need extra clamping pressure to close the gap. Apply glue to the core and lay down the edging with cauls and clamps. **B** Use the previous method to flush everything up with a saw and sharp block plane. **C** Complete the job with a light sanding.

PREPARE & MATCH THE VENEER

A We can now start to prepare our veneers. Before jointing, arrange these in a way that looks good by either slip matching, flip matching, or even book matching. **B** Don't forget to mark your pieces with numbered masking tape. **C** The full width of the tray is 13"; joint and join your veneers to get the full width plus an extra 1" or 1½". **D** Using the techniques described in Chapter 4, after jointing you should get a seamless joint for both the bottom and top pieces.

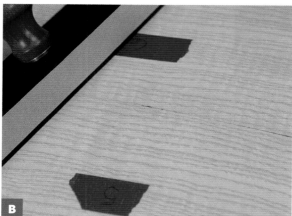

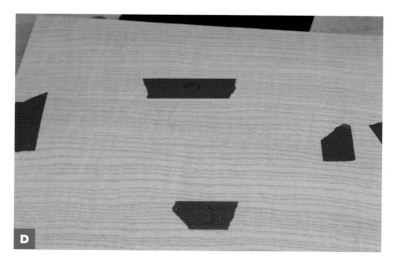

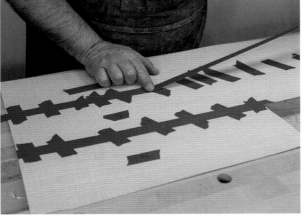

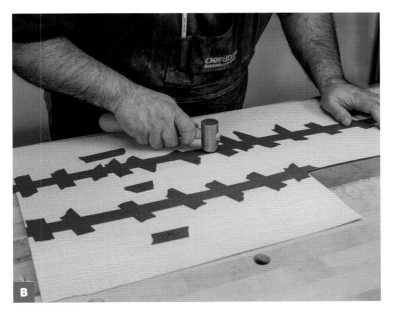

TAPE THE VENEER

A First, use masking tape on the glue side to secure the seams.
B Burnish the tape with a hammer to bind it up nicely.
C Flip the veneer over and apply the moistened veneer tape on the show side using your handmade tape dispenser (page 44). Lay the veneer between two pieces of MDF while it all dries. Repeat this process with the second piece of veneer.
D When the veneer tape is dry, peel away the masking tape from the glue side of the veneers, making sure it's clean and smooth.

GLUE THE VENEER

A Take one more pass at the edging and the surface of the MDF core to make sure everything is clean and smooth. Then, apply the adhesive to the core and cover it with the veneer. Remember to get a nice, even spread with no pools or dry spots. Place the thin, packing-taped caul on top along with the thick caul and flip it over on its back. Add glue, the second veneer sheet, and finally the last thin and thick cauls.

B Slip the whole assembly into the press and start to tighten down the press screws. **C** Only tighten down the screws that are directly over the veneer sandwich. Let this sit for at least three or four hours, but longer than that won't hurt. Remove the assembly from the press and prop it up overnight to 24 hours before doing any work on it.

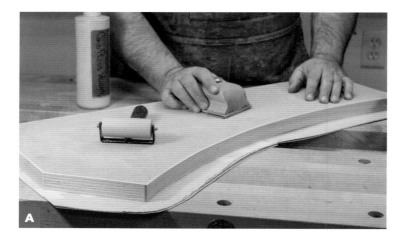

FLUSH THE EDGES OF THE TRAY

A With the tray fully glued up and cured, clean up the overhanging veneer by flushing it back to the edge banding. Using a sharp knife, cut away most of the overhang close to the edges. **B** Using the teeth on the side of a mill file, flush the veneer to the capping, making sure to file toward the center and not outward. Angle the file so it doesn't hit the other side. **C** Use a sponge to wet the veneer tape. Let it soak in before removing the tape. **D** Clean up any stubborn pieces that refuse to be lifted by using a scraper.

CLEAN UP THE TRAY

A Clean up the tray edges with a combination of planes, files, scrapers, and sandpaper. **B** For the curved front, start with a scraper. **C** Attach self-adhesive sandpaper to a ⅛" hardboard caul to follow the contours closely. **D** White ash can be brittle. If it does chip or crack, use a dental pick to carefully pry the veneer away from the core; add glue. **E** Seal loose veneer with glue and green binding tape. (Blue masking tape will work, but the holding power of the green tape is stronger). Use a smooth file or 180–220-grit sandpaper at 45° to blend the veneer into the solid wood edging.

TURN YOUR ATTENTION TO THE BOX

While the tray cures, start on the box. For the tray, the veneer didn't need to be cross-laminated because MDF does not have any grain.  However, for the box, make sure to cut the Baltic birch plywood core so the grain runs perpendicular to the veneers. Size the core larger than needed so it can be cleaned up after pressing.  Use the plywood cores as templates for the veneers and cut them with a sharp knife and a cutting mat. Don't throw away any pieces; use them to cap the edges with matching grain.  Remember to use masking tape when cutting veneer across the grain.  With the veneer cut, you're ready to press.  Place the pieces in the press, using the cauls from the tray pressing. Again, only tighten down the press screws that are directly over the top of the veneer sandwich. Remove the pieces after a few hours, prop them up, and let them fully cure before doing any cleanup. In a repeat of the previous steps, press the center divider and back panel of the box, letting them fully cure as well.

GET THE BOX PIECES READY

A For the box pieces, find the long edge with the least amount of overhang. **B** Use the teeth on the side of the file to flush up this edge. Clean it up further on the jointer. **C** Crosscut the ends to length and rip the pieces to width. **D** Use a sharp plywood blade and reinforce the cut line with masking tape that has been burnished down. **E** Move to a router table to cut dados for the side pieces so they will fit flush to the top and bottom. **F** Cut a dado in the center of the top and bottom pieces to accept the divider.

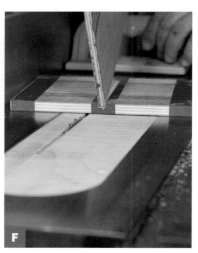

APPLY THE EDGES TO THE BOX

A Use the same figured black limba veneer and match the grain in order to cap the back and side edges of the top and bottom. Then use glue, masking tape, covered pine cauls, and clamps to secure it. **B** Mentioned earlier, one trick to ensure the veneer stays put during the initial clamping is to add a few drops of a medium or thick cyanoacrylate adhesive after applying the white glue. Hold it in position for a few seconds and it will hold while you apply cauls and clamps. Use this trick to ensure that grain lines or figured details stay aligned when applying clamping pressure.

REPAIRING EDGES IS EASY

On a small note, I wasn't happy with the placement of the veneer edging on one of the side pieces of the box. **A** It didn't quite match the top and I had another piece that would work much better. **B** Using a block plane with a sharp blade and a fine cut, I removed the edging and reapplied the better edge. This is one of the benefits of working with veneer. It's forgiving and very easy to make repairs to the edging.

ASSEMBLING THE BOX

Before putting the box together, sand the interior surfaces; they will be hard to reach later. Second, the back panel will be inset, so the center divider needs to be cut a little shorter than the depth of the box. **A** Glue up the box except for the center divider. It needs to move forward in order to cut the rabbet at the back of the box. Apply clamps and cauls and give it time to cure.

APPLY THE FRONT & BACK EDGING

B With the top, bottom, and sides veneered and edged, use short veneer pieces to edge the vertical surfaces on the front and back, including the front of the center divider. The rear of the center divider will be covered by the back panel and does not need any edging. **C** After glue cures on the front vertical edges, use a small square and a chisel for the straight lines. **D** Trim back the edging to make room for the top and bottom pieces.

E Do the same for vertical edging on the back of the box. **F** Joint one edge of veneer. **G** Cap off the top and bottom on both the front and back of the box.

CLEAN UP THE EDGING & INSTALL THE BACK PANEL

A After letting everything cure, clean up any overhang as done previously with a file and sandpaper. **B** Gently work across the piece. **C** For the veneered back panel, use a bearing router bit and cut a dado on the back of the box to accept it. **NOTE** Don't let the dado for the center divider in the top and bottom mess up any straight lines. Fill them in with scrap pieces or stop the router bit as you approach the dado. Square off the corners and trim until you can just tap the back in place. Use glue and clamp it in place.

THE FEET & THE FINISH

A To complete the tray, mill up some feet that are just short of the tray's width. They can be attached to the narrow end and to where the curve peaks out after applying a finish. Using a random-orbit sander under vacuum, sand the tray and the box's outer surfaces. Blend all the veneers into the edging at 45° with either a file or sandpaper. Apply the finish of your choice following the manufacturer's instructions. **B** After the finish has dried, using dowel centers and a square, glue and attach the feet. As another option, store-bought eet can work as well.

WRAPPING UP

There are options when completing this project, including omitting the box all together. However, I hope you build it because it will give you the experience of piecing and matching small strips of veneer to get a pleasing, continuous grain pattern. The box can be made with a drawer instead of the center divider. The drawer spans the opening of the box and can be made out of solid wood. It's basically another box. I ended up using some solid black limba to make a traditional dovetailed drawer. Yes, occasionally I use solid wood as well. (Shhh...don't tell anyone.)

CHAPTER 9

PLATFORM BOX

Be Like NASA: Harness the Power of Vacuum

Harnessing a vacuum to press veneers is my favorite method of veneering. It's like hiring Mother Nature as a subcontractor to do the work for you. Vacuum provides a tremendous amount of even pressure over large surfaces—including concave and convex forms—that would be difficult to achieve with typical clamping techniques. Depending on how high above sea level you reside, vacuum pumps can apply anywhere from 1100 to 1400 pounds per square foot (PSF). Trust me when I say that it's more than enough to get the job done!

THE CONCEPT

The first pressings I did in school were with a commercial press. I thought you needed 8' bags and commercial pumps that magically knew when to turn on and off. I was genuinely thrilled when I saw Roarockit's Thin Air Press kit (see page 144). Originally used to make skateboards, this manual pump vacuum kit is well suited to make fine furniture, and does as good a job at a fraction of the cost of other options.

We'll use the Roarockit kit to make a platform box. I thought we could create a bit of visual magic—similar to a piano keyboard—with some holly and a contrast of solid ebony. By adding zebrawood to the inside, a nice visual surprise awaits anyone opening the box. The black dyed veneer for the base creates a nice shadow line. Dyed veneer is a better option than staining veneer because the dye is typically infused throughout, while the stain can be sanded off.

While this project may seem difficult at first glance, it's very easy if you tackle one step at a time. In fact, the hardest part of the project is keeping the ebony dust off the holly veneer to maintain that crisp contrast line.

We'll start by pressing all the components and then capping the exposed substrate with either holly veneer or solid ebony banding. Rabbets and dados keep the joinery simple and the final assembly will happen after the finish is applied. Titebond Cold Press for Veneer is perfect for this job, but any PVA or water-based glue will work. When capping the edges, use white carpenters' glue because it dries translucent and does not create a dark visible glue line.

TOOLS & MATERIALS

- Tablesaw with crosscut fence
- Knife with sharp blade
- Blue masking and packing tape
- Hammer
- Vacuum press with cauls, platen, netting, pump, and bags
- Block plane
- Newspaper or kraft paper
- Polyvinyl acetate glue, such as Titebond Cold Press for Veneer

- Brayer
- File
- Jointer
- Clamps and cauls
- Random-orbit sander with vacuum
- Finish of choice
- (6) #5¾" flat-head wood screws
- Drill
- ⅛" microdowel

*If there are two parts that differ only by one measurement, such as a substrate and its veneer face (thickness, in this case), both are shown in one line with the differences in parentheses. Other columns in that line without a parenthetical option are the same for both parts.

PROJECT PLANS

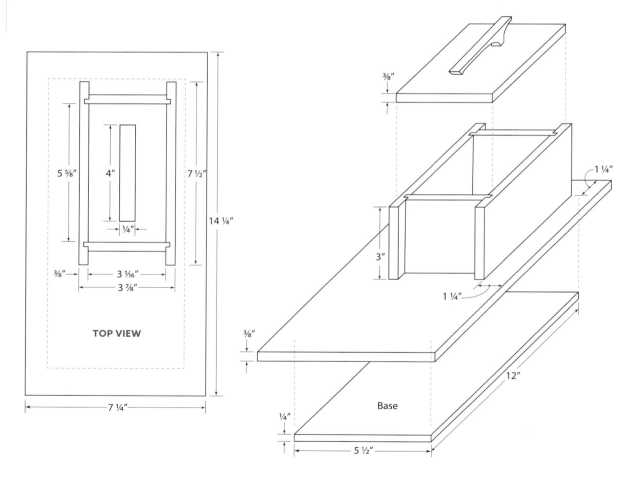

TOP VIEW

Base

CUT LIST

QTY	PIECE	MATERIAL	L	W	T
2 (4)	Box front and back cores (and faces)	Baltic birch plywood (Holly veneer)	7½"	3"	⅜" (<¹⁄₁₆")
2 (4)	Box side cores (and faces)	Baltic birch plywood (Holly veneer)	3⁷⁄₁₆"	3"	⅜" (<¹⁄₁₆")
1 (2)	Box lid core (and faces)	Baltic birch plywood (Holly veneer)	5⅜"	2 ¹³⁄₁₆"	⅜" (<¹⁄₁₆")
1 (2)	Platform core (and faces)	Baltic birch plywood (Holly veneer)	14"	7"	⅜" (<¹⁄₁₆")
1 (2)	Base core (and faces)	Baltic birch plywood (Black-dyed veneer)	12"	5½"	¼" (<¹⁄₁₆")
2	Inner lip core, long sides (and faces)	MDF or hardboard (Zebrawood veneer)	5⅝"	2¾"	⅛" (<¹⁄₁₆")
2	Inner lip core, short sides (and faces)	MDF or hardboard (Zebrawood veneer)	2 ¹³⁄₁₆"	2¾"	⅛" (<¹⁄₁₆")
2 (2)	Platform edging, short (and long)	Ebony	7" (14¼")	⅜"	⅛"
2 (2)	Base edging, short (and long)	Black-dyed veneer	5½" (12")	¼"	<¹⁄₁₆"
4	Box front and back edging, short sides	Holly veneer	3"	⅜"	<¹⁄₁₆"
2 (2)	Inner lip top edging, short (and long)	Zebrawood veneer	2 ¹³⁄₁₆" (5⅝")	⅛"	<¹⁄₁₆"
1	Box top edging	Holly veneer	7½"	3⅞"	<¹⁄₁₆"
2 (2)	Box lid edging, short (and long)	Ebony	2 ¹³⁄₁₆" (5⅝")	⅜"	⅛"
1	Handle	Ebony	4"	⅝"	¼"

GETTING STARTED

Inspect all your materials to make sure you have enough veneer and a bit more to complete the project. Always size the components a little wider and longer so that you have room to clean up edges, account for possible shifted veneers, and a bit more room to play with. Lumber stores will have "hobby size" sheets of Baltic birch coming in 2' x 4', and you'll be able to get a few boxes out of each sheet. Practice makes perfect after all, or maybe it just makes more gifts for those special people in your life. Also, pick up a 2' x 4' piece of ⅛" MDF or hardboard that is smooth on both sides, as we will use this not only for the internal lip, but also as cauls to press our veneers. To help manage the pressing of components, it is easier to press a larger panel and cut it up later into the smaller components. Instead of trying to press seven individual pieces, we can get away with five. (We just have to include enough length and width to allow for cleanup and what will go to waste from the blade kerf. A little bit more doesn't hurt either.) To achieve this, cut the ⅜"-thick Baltic birch to 4" x 16" for the front and back pieces. We can lump the lid in with the box sides, which will require a piece 13" x 3 ⅞". We will increase the required size for the platform and base by ½" on length and width. Make the piece for the internal lip 20" x 3 ⅛".

LAYING OUT & CUTTING THE VENEER

When laying out the pieces for the grouped components, remember to orient the grain on the plywood perpendicular to the direction of the grain on the veneer. It's an easy thing to overlook, but it's an important step to keep things in balance. Holly doesn't appear to have any visible grain lines, but upon closer inspection, you'll see them. The grain on the front and back of the box will run horizontally while the sides sport vertical lines. As a result, the grain appears to run along the platform, up the side of the box, across the lid, down the opposite side, and then back along the platform. It is even more visible with a stronger-grained veneer. You can really only achieve this with veneer. If solid wood was used, the components would fight each other with seasonal movement. **A** To cut the veneer to size, use a sharp knife. **B** Use the substrate pieces as templates. **C** Cut two pieces for each core, paying attention to your veneer. **D** Use masking tape where required to stop tearing and splitting.

Vacuum Pressing Caul

vacuum bag
⅛" hardboard
veneer
platen

substrate

When the caul is too big, vacuum pressure warps the caul, creating a gap in caul-veneer contact.

MAKE THE CAULS

After the veneers are cut, move on to the cauls. With the vacuum method of pressing, there is so much even pressure that thicker cauls are not required; thin cauls, such as ⅛" or ¼" hardboard, are more than adequate. **A** Size these no more than ¼" larger than the length and width of the substrate. **B** In the case of vacuum veneering, if there's too much of an overhang, the edges will not get pressed—the pressure from the bag will force the overhang down toward the platen, making just enough of a void near the edges to stop a good pressing. You can also size the cauls equal to what you're pressing to be sure you avoid this. **C** It's a good idea to sand down any sharp corners that might damage the vacuum bag. **D** One other treatment is to prepare a glue resist. Like the cauls in Chapter 8, you can use either packing tape or some Waxilit paste or a hard paste wax without silicone. You really don't want the cauls to become a permanent part of your piece.

TIME TO PREP FOR PRESSING

This is the stage where things get exciting.  **A** Cover your work surface with some newsprint and set up the vacuum bag, including the platen, netting, and pump. Tear some small strips of masking tape to hold everything together. **B** Mix your glue, grab your spreader, and remove any masking tape from your veneer cutting session. **NOTE** I felt comfortable pressing three components and then doing a second pressing with the remaining two. If you are unsure, do a dry run to gauge your timing. However, there is absolutely nothing wrong with pressing one or two pieces at a time. **C** Spread your glue on the substrate. There should be no dry spots or pools of glue. Go right to the edges to ensure the veneer is adhered very well. **D** Cover the substrate with veneer and add a caul. **E** Flip over and repeat. **F** Use four of those short masking tape pieces to tape the four sides from top caul to bottom caul.

BAG & SEAL THE SANDWICHES

A Slip the sandwich in the bag and repeat with however many components you want to press. Fifteen minutes can be long or short. Carefully arrange the sandwiches on the platen so that the bag can close around each component. While the bag doesn't have to enclose each piece down to the platen, some space between them is good. **B** Add the breather netting connecting all the sandwiches and valve. **C** Ensure you get a good seal at the opening. I find the most common area of leaks to be where the sealing tape meets the factory seams on each end.

CREATE THE VACUUM

It's time for some elbow grease. **A** Start pumping and within short order you'll feel more resistance in the pump. You'll also see the bag close around the cauls. You'll want the bag to very firmly seal and press around your sandwich. **B** Write the time on a piece of masking tape and stick it to the bag. At a minimum, leave it "cooking" in the bag for at least two to three hours. Longer, or even overnight, is not a problem. **C** Double-check the seal before you walk away; check on the bag periodically to make sure it is holding vacuum and there are no leaks. Typically, I try to time my pressings for late morning or early afternoon and remove them late in the evening.

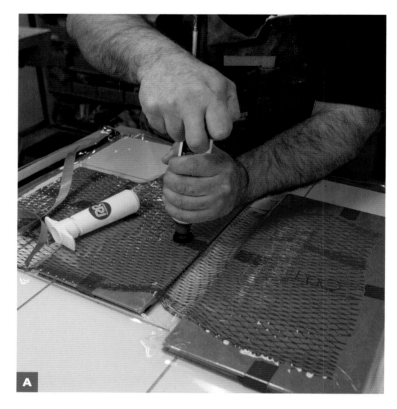

A

B

C

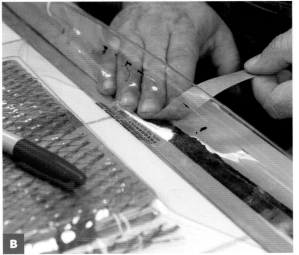

OPEN THE BAG

Time to open the bag and see how we made out. Toggle the button on the valve stem and let the air back in. **A** Using the blunt end of a marker, start to unseal the bag. **B** Place the paper strip back on the sealing tape and remove your pressings. **NOTE** Chances are, you'll see some shifted veneer and what seems like stretched veneer. It's very tempting to bend and break the overhanging veneer, but hold off for now. Why?

Well, glue doesn't fully cure in a vacuum because the moisture needs to evaporate from glue and there is no air movement in a vacuum. **C** Prop each component up and let it rest with surrounding air movement at least overnight, if not for 24 hours or longer. We don't want to just lay all the pieces on a flat surface, one on top of the other. Remember, be patient and give yourself every opportunity to do good work.

COMPLETE THE REMAINING ROUNDS OF PRESSING

While the first components are fully curing, complete the rest of your pressings.  **A** Prep your glue, grab your spreader, and remove the masking tape from your veneer. **B** Spread your glue on the substrate, cover with veneer, and add a caul. Remember that there should be no dry spots or pools of glue. Go right to the edges to ensure the veneer is adhered very well. **C** Flip it over and repeat. Apply short masking tape pieces to the four sides from top caul to bottom caul.

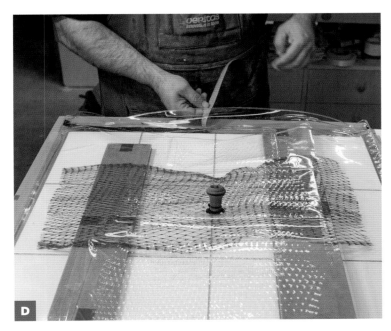

D Slip the sandwiches in the bag, add the breather netting, and ensure a good seal on the bag. **E** Start pumping to create the vacuum. **F** Don't forget to mark the time.

TIME TO CLEAN UP THE COMPONENTS

We need to get true rectangles before we can start to cut our components out of the larger pieces. This is easily accomplished as long as we have one clean edge. **A** Your sandwiches will probably come out with some shifting and a few with an overhang of veneer on the edges. Look at each component and find one long edge that has the least amount of veneer overhang or possibly none. **B** Using the teeth on the edge of the file, push toward the substrate at an angle and cut the veneer as described in Chapter 2. Work both sides of that one long edge. **C** Use a power jointer to clean it up some more. **D** Repeat this step for all the pieces.

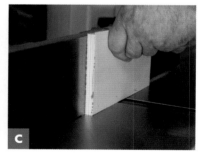

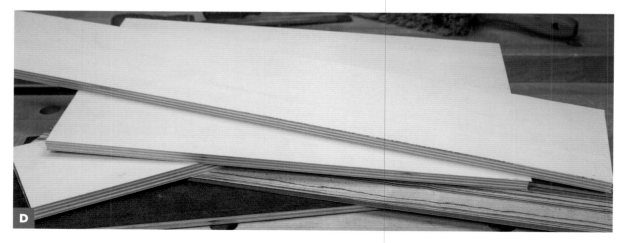

CUT THE PIECES TO SIZE

Cut everything except the lid. To ensure a nice tight fit, it will be sized separately after the box is assembled. **A** Use a tablesaw and fence to rip your pieces to width. **B** Then use the tablesaw to trim down the pieces. **C** A crosscut sled is handy to trim the pieces to length.

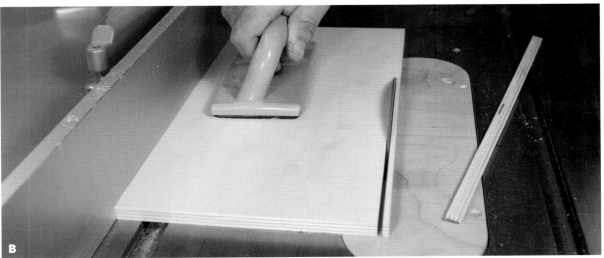

EDGE THE PLATFORM

For the platform edging, mill up some ebony edging that is ⅛" thick and approximately ½" wide. You'll need two pieces that are about ½" longer than the width of the platform and two pieces ½" longer than the length. I chose to glue the short ends first as the front and back edging will hide the butt joint. Ebony does a good job of hiding joints anyway, which is one of the reasons I like to use it. Using clamps and pine cauls, covered with either packing tape or blue masking tape, glue the edging to the platform. Make sure it stands proud of both surfaces and there is enough "fat" to trim off the ends. As I mentioned before, I prefer to use white glue because it dries translucent and does not create a visible glue line.  **A** Once the platform is out of the clamps, trim up the width pieces. Start by cutting the "ears" back so that just ⅛" remains.  **B** Use a block plane with tape diagonally across the front corner that will ride on the veneered surface of the platform. As you'll recall, this will prop it up so it only cuts the solid ebony edging and not the veneer.  **C** Pay attention. When you get close to flush, you'll start to see some glue in the shavings. This is an indication to slow down. Keep feeling with your fingers and stop when you are almost flush. A little proud is fine; we still need to do some sanding in order to clean the surfaces.

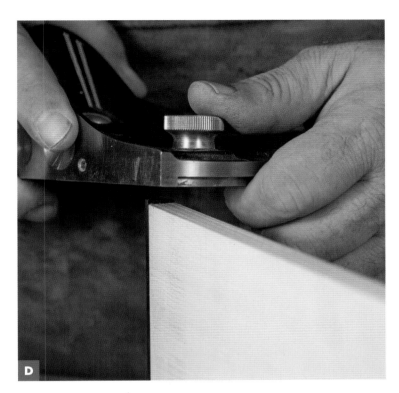

D Remove the tape from the block plane and flush the ebony ends to the bare plywood. Ebony is brittle, so take your time with light cuts. Don't go back and forth, but rather toward the plywood, lifting on the backstroke. **E** With the short edging done, focus on the long edges with more glue, cauls, and clamps; clean it up once the glue has cured. Work the remaining edges in the same manner described here.

PREPARE THE EDGING FOR THE BASE, BOX & INNER LIP

Gluing veneer edging is no different from solid wood edging. Add glue to the plywood or MDF and use cauls covered with tape. You shouldn't need a lot of clamping force but look for a bit of squeeze-out all around. **A** Similar to the edging of the platform, apply the edging to short ends of the base using black dyed veneer and your collection of cauls, glue, and clamps. **B** Cut your veneer edging longer and wider than the actual pieces. Remember to put enough glue on the edges because later we will flush them with a file. Apply the same edging treatment to the short ends of the front and back pieces of the box. **C** Once the glue has cured, trim any extra length with a sharp knife, leaving ears that are about ⅛" proud. **D** Wrap the tip of a mill file with a few layers of blue tape. Place the covered tip on the veneered face and use the teeth on the edge once more to flush the veneered capping. Remember to push and cut toward the center, not backward. Work your way through all the pieces.

E For the ears, leave the tape on the tip of the file and cut the excess as before. **F** Leave a nice, clean edge. **G** Glue one long piece of zebrawood onto what will become the top of the inner lip. **H** The bottom of this piece as well as the sides and bottom of the box do not receive any edging. There really is no need for it.

CREATE JOINERY FOR THE BOX

It's time for some joinery for the box. Lay out the pieces and mark them with a cabinetmakers' triangle. Using a crosscut sled and a couple of stops, cut dados ½" in from the ends of the front and back pieces. The dados should be along the 3" height and about ³⁄₁₆" wide and ³⁄₁₆" deep. Next, create rabbets on the box sides that will fit into the newly created dados. In order for the joinery to come together, don't bottom out the rabbets. A little bit of a gap is perfectly fine and will be hidden by the veneer edging. **A** Make sure everything fits together. **B** Clean things up; blend the veneer edges of each piece of the box toward each other. Use a smooth file and/ or sandpaper with a chamfering motion. This helps hide the small seams between the two adjacent points. Use 180-grit sandpaper on a random-orbit sander under vacuum to sand the platform. Sanding under vacuum will keep the ebony dust from getting into the holly veneer's grain. Change the sandpaper often if you're not getting a clean line between the two colors. Remember, you only have so much veneer to work with. Use the random-orbit sander again for the rest of the components or handsand with a block. Apply glue to the dados. Paying attention to your triangle, assemble the box with cauls and clamps and let it cure for a few hours.

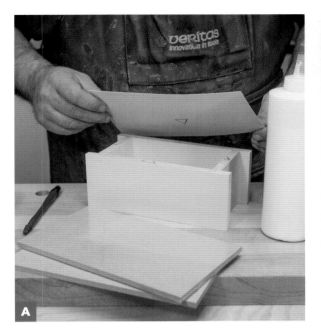

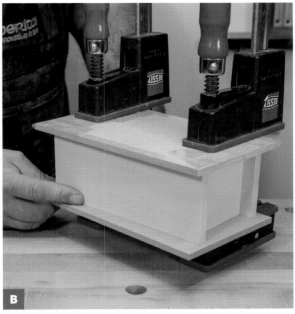

APPLY THE TOP EDGING TO THE BOX

A Once out of the clamps, cut a piece of holly veneer slightly overhanging the edges on the top of the box. **B** Use your trusty glue, cauls, and clamps to attach this piece to the box top. **C** After the glue has completely cured, cut out the center from the top of the box, turn it on its side, and, using a combination of knives and files, trim the veneer flush with the top edges. **D** Continue. By now you're probably getting pretty good at this. As long as you've applied enough glue, you shouldn't have any trouble.

MAKE THE INSIDE LIP & BOX TOP

A Now for the internal lip and the box top: cut the zebrawood panel so that you get continuous grain around the interior. **B** Cut the pieces a little long on the tablesaw, then use a shooting board to get that perfect fit. **C** The front and back pieces will run the full width. The left and right short sides will capture the long pieces by pushing the ends into the corners of the box's interior. Once the components are sized, you'll glue them in after you affix the box to the platform. **D** For the box top, measure and trim the lid, keeping in mind we will cap it with ⅛"-thick ebony edging all around. Later, use a handplane or sandpaper on the edging so the top drops in and rests on the zebrawood lip for the perfect fit. **E** Shape a handle out of ebony to your liking. (I found this pattern pleasing and nice to hold.) A purchased knob will work fine too. **F** Using the same methods that you used before to apply the edging, glue, clamp, trim, and repeat until all four edges of the box lid are done.

FINAL FINISH & ASSEMBLY

Start your clean up by sanding any scratches or blemishes away.  It's easier to apply a finish before final assembly, so mask off areas to be glued, like the box position, the underside of the platform, and the top of the base. For the finish, a shellac can be substituted, or an application of fine furniture wax will work. Just follow the manufacturer's instructions for the finish you choose. After the finish has dried, remove any tape and glue and prepare to screw the box to the platform. Set the box on top of the platform in the top left area. A good place is 1 ¼" from the back and from the left side of the platform. 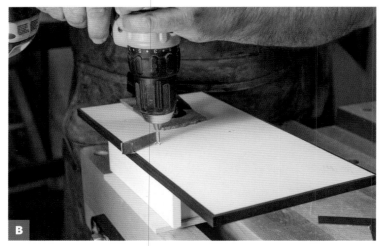 Clamp it to the platform and flip it over with the platform resting on the box. Drill pilot holes for the #5 x ¾" flat-head wood screws into the bottom of the platform. Measure twice, even three times, before drilling.  Drive the six screws from below through your pilot holes. Take your time with this, as you want to make sure you hit the center of the walls on the box. When this is done, attach the base to the bottom of the platform with glue and clamps; while that cures, attach the handle to the lid. A great way to attach a shop-made handle is with a ⅛" microdowel into both the lid and knob.

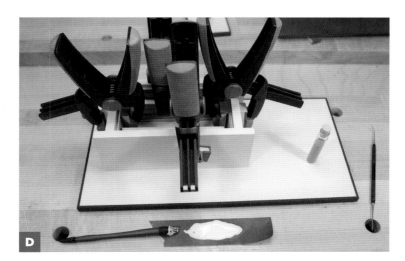

D At this point, with the box affixed to the platform, don't forget to glue in the zebrawood interior pieces. Depending on the type of clamp you use, a few grains of sand will make sure that the clamps don't shift the internal pieces. **E** The finished box and platform will look great no matter what you decide.

WRAPPING UP

There are lots of ways to customize this box. Pick edging that is similar to your veneer or use a contrasting tone like this project. Change the size of the box to suit the function of the box. In the end, the design and techniques for this project are only achievable with veneer. The sides of the box could not run their grain perpendicular to the front and back if it were made out of solid wood.

Vacuum veneering with a kit like this is well within your technology know-how and budgetary reach. And it doesn't just have to be used for box parts. It can just as easily be panels, curved work or a skateboard. While this initial kit may limit the size of your projects, larger bag sizes are available on their own or as part of a kit. As long as you take care of your bag, you'll have it around to veneer with for quite some time.

ROAROCKIT VACUUM KITS

These kits are available at a variety of woodworking stores as well as the Roarockit website.

A The Thin Air Press used in this chapter comes with everything you need to start pressing veneers except for the materials. It includes a vacuum bag with seal, a one-way valve, a pump, breather netting, extra tape for sealing, and well-written instructions. A trip to the company's website provides lots of tips and tricks to help you along. A variety of bag sizes are available individually or in kit form. Extra seal tape, netting, and spare valve caps can also be purchased. For most of my work, the kit sized 26" x 28", along with the next size up at 36" x 52", are perfect. It might not seem possible to generate the same pressure with a manual pump that you would with an electrical pump, but— believe it or not—the opposite is true. It's not difficult either and might provide just the right amount of exercise to make your doctor happy. In fact, you'll probably only need about 30 to 45 seconds of exercise to reach the proper vacuum.

B When using the bag, make sure to keep sharp objects away from the vinyl. Keep the sealing tape clean and sticky by replacing the paper strip as soon as you unseal the bag. Sand all outer edges of cauls and soften the corners. Do this on all the cauls so that it doesn't matter which goes on the top or the bottom.

C The breather netting is a way of channeling the air inside a sealed bag toward the valve. You need to place the netting under the valve and spread it out over the top cauls of what you are pressing. The netting comes in a tube form. I cut it in half, then cut it once more to the length needed. It can be stretched out, so the netting

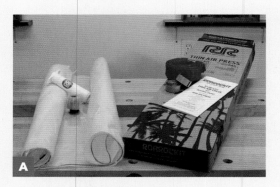

included in your kit will go a long way.

NOTE The reason I use a top caul on my pressings is to prevent the netting from making an impression on the veneer that will need to be sanded out later. Remember, you only have so much veneer to work with.

You'll need a flat base, also known as a platen, to use with this type of kit. A piece of melamine ⅝" or ¾" thick works great. For the bag in this kit, a 24" x 24" piece is ideal. Don't size the platen to the same size as the bag, but rather leave some room for the bag to collapse around it.

D To help evacuate the air toward the valve along with the breather netting, cut ⅛" channels that are approximately ⅛" deep across the top face of the platen. This is very easily accomplished on a tablesaw. Space them roughly 6" to 8" apart.

E Round the edges of the melamine using a trim router and roundover bit.

F Just to be on the safe side, use a sanding block with 120-grit sandpaper to smooth out the corners and any rough spots. Most woodworking glues won't stick to melamine (or the bag for that matter), but there is nothing wrong with applying a bit of Waxilit or other hard paste wax to the surface.

Among the several bags I have from Roarockit, I've replaced the sealing tape on several occasions. Replace the tape when it no longer seals; if you replace the paper strip when unsealing the bag it will go a long way to maintaining it. Repairs to the bag are very easy to make.

(continued on next page)

ROAROCKIT VACUUM KITS *(continued)*

G To find stubborn small leaks, place a piece of cardboard inside the bag, seal it, and create a vacuum. Don't forget the netting around the valve.

H Spray water over the bag and look for a dark spot. You've found your leak.

I Repairs can be made with packing tape or even a vinyl repair kit.

J I've used a piece of an old bag and vinyl cement in extreme cases. Read and adhere to the cautions of vinyl cement; although it is great for vinyl repairs, it is far from good for you. A well-ventilated area and respiratory protection is required.

K If you feel you're not getting a good seal around the valve, a mist of water will fill any gaps that could be there. If your shop is dusty like mine, I tend to give the valve a quick misting before starting.

If you're careful handling your bag, it will give you plenty of use for all sorts of projects. Just make sure to take care of the seams and keep sharp objects at a distance. And never forget: don't run with scissors.

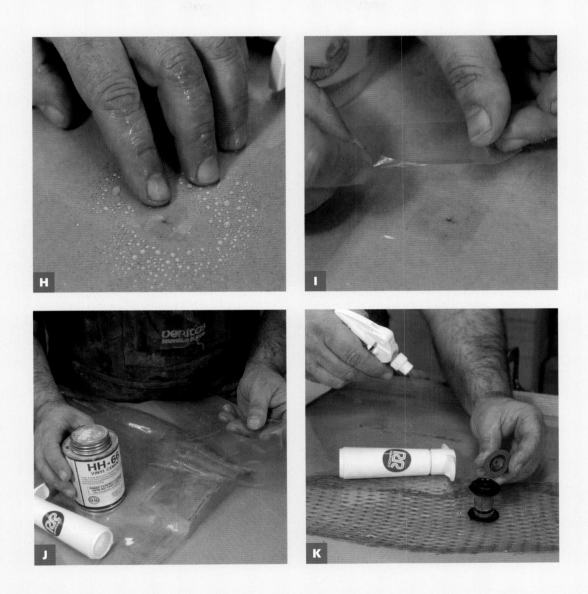

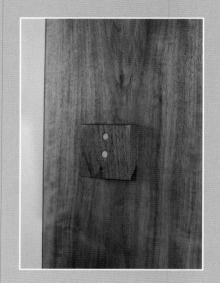

CHAPTER 10

CURVED WALL PANEL

It's Not All Straight Lines: Experiment with Making Curves

Yes, it's hip to be square, but sooner or later you'll want to try to make something that's not square, rectangular, or straight. Veneer is the perfect medium to delve into making curved pieces. You can add some curvy character to a piece of furniture. Perhaps a guitar or a ukulele would be fun to make. Heck, you can add a nice curve to a skateboard deck. If you keep your eyes open, you'll see curves everywhere.

THE CONCEPT

While this is the most involved project, it's very achievable with the methods used in the previous chapters. Using vacuum pressure, we'll make a decorative curved wall panel with an added mirror and shelf for functionality.

Another valuable tip I received in school was to look everywhere for ideas. Believe it or not, this design came out of a garden center. In addition to the plants, the store had a section with bird houses and other accessories. In one corner, they had a half-circular water trough that could double as a raised planter when elevated on legs. The idea for this design popped into my head because they had it propped up against the wall to its full height. Hence, the Curved Wall Panel was born.

This project demonstrates the full power of vacuum veneering when you have an easy-to-use, well-set-up system. Pay a visit to Vacuum Pressing Systems (VPS) (*www.vacupress.com*), where you can research vacuum pumps, bag options, and accessories like vacuum clamping and adhesives. For this project, we're using the Compact 300 VacuPress pump and a blown polyurethane bag with a pressing capacity of 49" x 97". This system makes it easy to vacuum press not only flat panels but also curved projects.

Bending wood in this manner is accurate, reliable and repeatable. Curved doors and other bends are also very achievable when building a form and pressing over it. The extra steps of adding backer veneer are worth it when you see the final outcome. These bends are very strong and stable. Making curves like this out of solid wood would be a problem due to seasonal expansion and contraction. I hope you try bending wood in this fashion because it's not as hard as it looks.

TOOLS & MATERIALS

- Vacuum press with platen, bag, and pump
- Drill and screws
- Hammer
- Chisel
- Tablesaw with crosscut sled and MDF sled
- Router with roundover and bearing pattern bit
- Block plane, sanding equipment of choice, and spindle sander
- Scrap MDF for template station
- Bandsaw
- Glues and brayer
- Square
- Pin or brad nailer
- Blue masking, packing, and veneer tape
- J roller
- Knife with sharp blade
- Clamps
- Dowels
- Newspaper or kraft paper
- Drying supports
- Custom-shaped rigid pink insulation sanding blocks
- Straightedge and angle finder

See bending form project plans on pages 182–183.

PROJECT PLANS

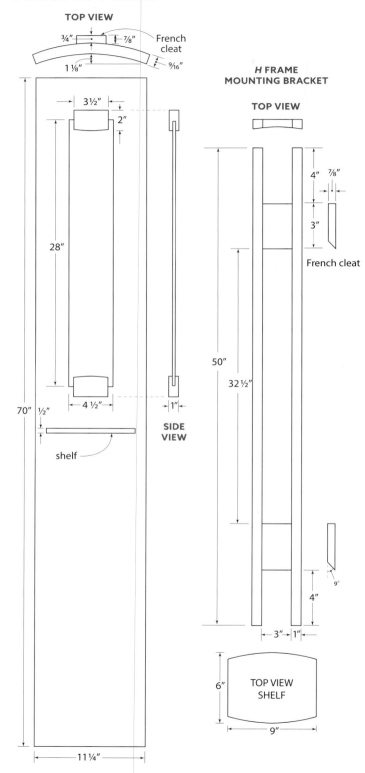

TOP VIEW

¾"   ⅞"   French cleat

1⅛"   ⁹⁄₁₆"

3½"

2"

28"

70"   ½"

4½"   1"

SIDE VIEW

shelf

H FRAME MOUNTING BRACKET

TOP VIEW

4"   ⅞"

3"

French cleat

50"

32½"

9°

4"

3"   1"

6"

TOP VIEW SHELF

9"

11¼"

CUT LIST

QTY	PIECE	MATERIAL	L	W	T
2 (2)	Panel core (and faces)	Bendable plywood	72" (70")	12"	5mm (<1⁄16")
3	Panel backer veneers	Backer veneer	70"	12"	<1⁄16"
2 (2)	Panel edging, short (and long)	Solid imbuia	11¼" (70")	9⁄16"	1⁄8"
1 (2)	Shelf core (and faces)	MDF (Claro walnut cluster burl veneer)	9"	6"	½" (<1⁄16")
2 (1)	Shelf edging, sides (and front)	Claro walnut cluster burl veneer	4½" (9¼")	½"	<1⁄16"
2	French cleats	Solid walnut	3"	3"	7⁄8"
2	H frame sides	Solid walnut	50"	1"	7⁄8"
2	H frame brackets	Solid walnut	4¾"	3"	¾"
2	Mirror clips	Solid walnut	3½"	2"	1"
1	Mirror	Mirror	28"	4½"	6mm

*If there are two parts that differ only by one measurement, such as a substrate and its veneer face (thickness, in this case), both are shown in one line with the differences in parentheses. Other columns in that line without a parenthetical option are the same for both parts.

A

B

C

MAKE A PLATEN & PREP THE SYSTEM

In order to get the system ready for vacuum veneering, you'll need to make a platen and a bending form to press the veneer sandwich. For this project, you can make one that is approximately 7' long by 24" wide. You'll find that after making a variety of projects, you'll have a variety of platens that you can simply pull out and use.

A Drill a hole sized and located on the platen following the instructions of the vacuum press. **B** Hammer in the plastic bushing. **C** Cut off any excess.

D Next, as we did in the previous chapter, use a tablesaw or a track saw to cut kerfs into the top of the platen to allow air to be channeled toward the bushing and, ultimately, the pump. A router with a fence could also be used. **E** Use a trim router and a roundover bit to soften all the edges and follow up with some 120-grit sandpaper. Complete a dry run of the system to make sure everything works as expected. Bags of this size will come open at both ends and closures can be used anywhere along its more than 8' length.

A WORD ABOUT VACUUM SYSTEMS

There are many options when selecting a vacuum system for your shop. Vacuum pumps have varying cubic feet per minute (CFM) ratings and different rates at which they can evacuate the air out of a bag. Give some thought to what you're most interested in making and pick a system that works best for those types of projects. For instance, it wouldn't make sense to buy a small pump for projects that require a large bag. The specific adhesives would more than likely set and be ineffective by the time the pump had evacuated all the air out of the bag.

As you're thinking about systems, there are also different options for bags beyond the size. Vacuum bags can be made of vinyl or polyurethane material, but recently VPS has released a line of blown polyurethane bags. Vinyl vacuum bags are cost effective and are a good choice for the hobbyist, but they aren't as strong, and a little extra care is needed to prevent damage. On the other hand, polyurethane bags, while more expensive, are sturdier with greater elasticity and puncture resistance. The newly launched blown polyurethane bags offer an in-between option with regard to cost, puncture resistance, and elasticity.

Don't be unnerved by the thought of purchasing a vacuum press and bags. The instructions for setting up the system are very well written and thoroughly cover important steps like making the platen, hooking up the hose, and making repairs if they're required. Aside from the platen, which we need to make, a good vacuum pressing system can be set up in minutes.

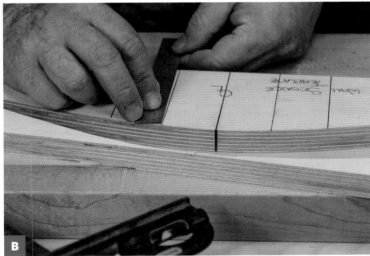

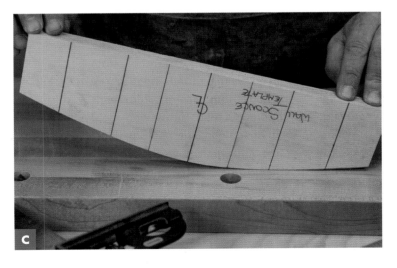

TEMPLATES FOR THE BENDING FORM

A lot of pressure will be applied in this project—approximately 1400 pounds per square foot at 500 feet above sea level—and the forms need to be strong. This sturdy design calls for the base, ribs, and spacers to be made of MDF with a skin of 5mm bendable plywood.

See cut list, rib template, and project plans on pages 182–183. Begin by making a template so that all the ribs will be perfectly matched (or use the one on page 182).  Start with a 13" piece of ½" plywood that has straight and parallel edges. Find the center and mark it clearly. It's very important to keep track of the center of all the components and transfer them from one to the other. Hammer two nails partway near the edges of the plywood and 1½" down from the top. Use a thin piece of wood to create a smooth curve by pushing it up toward the top and against the nails. The center should be 3¾", and the two edges 2 ⅜". Use a bandsaw to trim close to the line and a disc sander to make the curve true and clean. **NOTE** Any imperfections in the template will be duplicated into the ribs. Drawing equidistant lines from the bottom up using a square will make sure we have an accurate curve. Place it on edge on a flat surface and roll it back and forth to check for any inconsistencies.

MAKE THE RIBS FOR THE BENDING FORM

Set up a station to accurately attach and detach the template from each piece of MDF using some scrap MDF to create 90° corner. The pattern is 13", so cut the strips of MDF to this length. Size them a little wider than the pattern for cutting the curve and you're ready to mass-produce the 28 ribs needed (plus a few extra for good measure.) **A** Use countersink and pilot bits to drill and then attach the template to a piece of MDF with three screws. **B** Cut the MDF close to the template with a bandsaw, but avoid cutting the template. **C** This is where the extra width helps. Stay as far away from the template as you are comfortable with. **D** Use a bearing pattern bit on your router to cut the MDF flush to the template. **E** Before separating the tandem, place a mark on one side of both pieces to help line up the ribs when assembling the form. This will make sure that all ribs are an identical match. Repeat this process until all the MDF ribs are cut. **F** Clean them up by de-burring any holes from the screws.

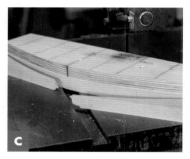

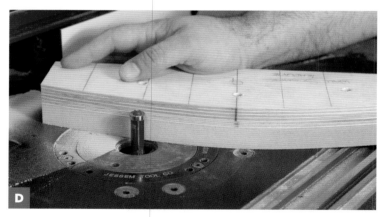

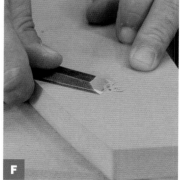

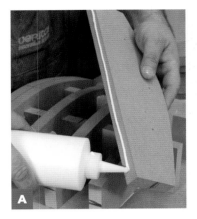

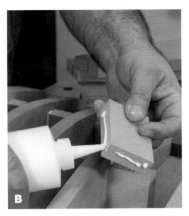

PUT THE FORM TOGETHER

Cut up some 2"-wide and 2½"-long pieces of MDF to be used as spacers. Gather them along with the ribs, a bottle of glue, a square, and either a pin or brad nailer. Set the base of the form on your workbench. Set up a fence on one long side of the base for registering the ribs. A little bit of masking tape will make sure any squeeze-out won't permanently attach the fence to the form. Set up another fence at one end of the form to keep things straight and square. **A** Apply glue to add ribs to the base. **B** Add spacers too, so the ribs are kept 2" apart. **C** Double up the ribs on the ends for a bit of extra strength against the pressure of the bag. Transfer your center mark to the outer rib and down the outside. Apply glue, wiggle it in place, add spacers, and check for square and alignment. Keep track of your mark on the side of each rib and make sure they are all facing the same way out. Work at a steady pace, checking often for accuracy (maybe every two or three ribs), and adjust accordingly. **D** You don't have to, but there's nothing wrong with driving pins into every rib and spacer combination. **E** You should have no problem keeping the ribs square straight up and down. The potential misalignment that might creep in is the distance from the end to each side of the rib. Check this constantly. As you progress, don't forget to transfer your centerline to the last rib and down its outside face.

ADD THE BENDABLE PLYWOOD

Once the ribs have been glued in, cut a piece of bendable plywood as long as your form and about 12" wide. Find center on both ends and mark this accurately. Set up the vacuum bag and pump and get ready to press the form in the bag. Sand any sharp edges that may contact the vacuum bag with a sanding block and 120-grit sandpaper. 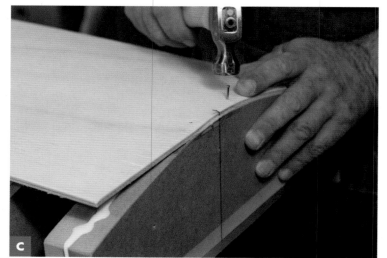 **A** Apply a bead of glue over each rib. **B** Put the bendable plywood skin on top and center it. **C** Drive in a pair of nails below the surface at each end to make sure it doesn't shift. **D** Slip it into the bag and let it "cook" for at least six hours if not longer. I usually leave forms like this in the bag overnight.

COMPLETE THE BENDING FORM

A After removing the form, scrape off any dried glue and re-sand any sharp areas that could puncture our bag. **B** Attach a layer of packing tape over the whole bend so that any pressings will not be permanently attached when completed. **C** Use a *J*-roller to press the clear tape down to the bendable plywood. **NOTE** Do the same for the inside surface of the remaining piece of bendable plywood that will be your top caul. Don't forget these important steps of applying packing tape.

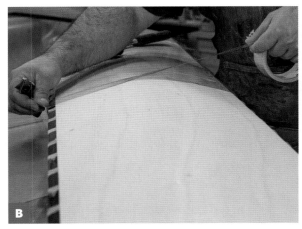

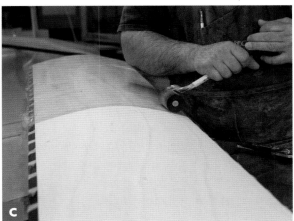

THE NEED FOR BACKER VENEER

Remember the importance of cross lamination when veneering. Since some of the earlier projects in this book included MDF with no grain, this wasn't a necessary step. For this project, if the two pieces of bendable plywood were simply glued together under the veneer, their grain would run the same way and would lead to problems. As a result, backer veneer is needed to complete the component sandwich. We will also need backer veneer on the sandwich sides. The grain of the show veneer runs in the same direction as the bendable plywood stack. Best of all, the addition of veneers and glue add to the strength of the finished piece.

PREPARE THE BACKER VENEER

Since the panel will be made of two sheets of bendable plywood, make three sheets of cross-laminated veneer to sandwich around them. When buying backer veneer, try buying sheets that have clean parallel edges; this saves time cleaning them up in preparation to be joined. To make up three sheets of backer veneer, use the techniques of taping used earlier in the book to get them ready for gluing.  Measure each piece 11½" wide to match the width of the bendable plywood. **B** Cut it with a utility knife. **C** For the backer veneer, an invisible seam isn't necessary, but you'll still want a very good one. Any small imperfections will be hidden by the show veneers. **D** Apply the masking tape to the glue side of two sheets of backer veneer. **E** Apply veneer tape on the show side. An exception is made on the third sheet because it's glued between the two pieces of bendable plywood. **F** Use three-hole veneer tape so that there is wood-to-wood contact through the holes.

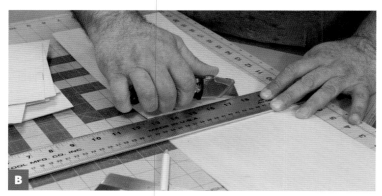

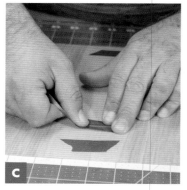

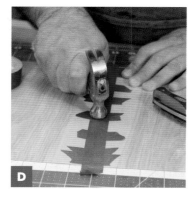

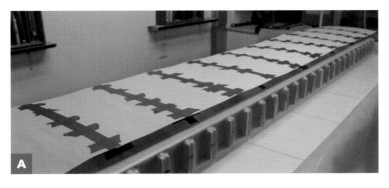

GET READY TO PRESS

A The backer veneer sheets should be as long and maybe a little wider than the core pieces. The core pieces will be as long as your form and approximately 11½" wide. In fact, make the outer of the two core pieces a little wider to reach completely around the curve.

MAKE SURE EVERYTHING IS CENTERED

Before applying the glue, make sure the veneers and core stay centered on the form. We'll use dowels as locating pins for consequent pressings. While cut oversized, there isn't much room to fix an off-center pressing. **B** To keep things aligned, place the backer veneer sheets, two pieces of bendable plywood, and the top caul in the form. Center everything and clamp both ends to hold everything down. Transfer the center lines on the edge of all the pieces. On one end, place the cabinetmaker's triangle to orient the core correctly on subsequent pressings. Drill a ⅜" hole down through the stack and into the bending form. Go deep, approximately 2" into the form. Repeat for the other end of the assembly. **C** Apply glue to a dowel and drive it home. Trim the height so that it is below the stack when assembled. The bag under vacuum will push the top caul down further. **D** Add a bit of a wax as a glue resist to help remove the pressings.

MIX THE GLUE & DO A DRY RUN

For glue, I used Unibond One from Vacuum Pressing Systems. Use your shop-made mixer (page 38), chucked into your drill, to mix the glue. Ensure the solids are spread through-out. Open and assembly time is approximately 15 minutes, but there is nothing wrong with pressing the core in steps. Do a dry run. If you can apply the glue, add the backer veneers, and slip it all into the bag before the time is up, follow the next steps. If you feel that you don't have enough time, do a bunch of "mini pressings" as described in the note at the end of these steps.

APPLY THE GLUE & "COOK"

Cover your workbench with paper and gather glue, rollers, spreaders, and the individual components of the core. **A** Remove any blue tape from the veneer sheets and place one onto the bending form.

SPRINGBACK

Springback is when the piece pulls away from the exact shape of the form when released from a pressing. Where the bend is more radical or tighter, you can experience some springback using PVA adhesives. In Chapter 3, we talked about what woodworkers refer to as "cold creep" because these glues don't dry rock hard and there is some flexibility.

Since the curve for the panel is very mild, any springback will be minimal, maybe 1/16", if it occurs at all. PVA adhesives for veneer like Unibond One and Titebond's Cold Press for Veneer will dry a little more rigid than white glue, but there could still be some springback. If it exceeds a small measurement, we might not be able to use the form to press the inner face veneer. In this instance, you would press the inner face with some bendable plywood, the veneer, and our core. The outer face gets pressed as normal.

B Place the inner bendable plywood core on your bench and apply the glue. Apply enough to cover the surface, but not so much that pools develop. A thin, even, and full-coverage coat is all that is required. Excess glue will not get pushed out and will form ripples in the finished piece. (I still usually end up scraping a lot off. By now, I have probably paid for a few Titebond engineers' children's educations.) When you've covered the surface, flip it over onto the form and apply glue to the other side.

Add the second backer sheet— the one with the three-hole veneer tape—over the dowels on the form. **C** Add glue to the next sheet of bendable plywood, flip it, and place it on the form. Add more glue. Add the final backer sheet. **D** Place the outer caul over the whole stack. **E** Add a strip of packing tape to the ends to hold everything in place. **F** Slip everything into the bag exactly like your rehearsal, seal the opening, and turn on the vacuum. Write the time on a piece of masking tape and place it on the bag. Let this "cook" for at least six hours. Don't forget to wash your rollers and spreaders.

NOTE Mini pressing sequence: Press the bendable plywood pieces with the backer veneer between them. Leave this in for approximately 45 minutes. Working at a steady pace, remove the assembly and then add glue and the inner backer sheet and press for 45 minutes. Finally, add glue and the outer backer veneer sheet and press this for the full duration of at least six hours.

REMOVE THE CORE

A While the sandwich is pressing, make supports covered with a soft material like cork or leather to support the core so air can circulate around it while it fully cures for 24 hours. **B** When the pressing has cured, remove the veneer tape by wetting with a moist sponge. **C** Peel it off. Clean up any rough spots with sandpaper. The outside of the curve can be sanded easily with a sanding block or flexible sanding sponges. **D** For the inside curve, make custom blocks out of rigid pink insulation. Attach 120-grit sandpaper with masking tape to the inside curve and run a small block of pink insulation back and forth until the curves match. Make several. **E** Use a light coating of spray adhesive to attach 220-grit sandpaper to the block and use it to clean up any rough spots or inconsistencies. We want a smooth layer for the show veneers.

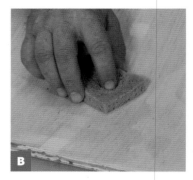

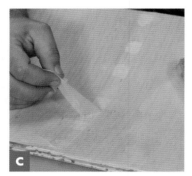

PREPARE THE SHOW VENEERS

A Center the show veneers over the bending form and drill holes for the centering dowels. **B** Use masking tape and a sharp knife to widen the holes so that they don't bind during the pressing. **C** To get them to width, put the veneer on the bending form and place the caul over top. Use a pencil to trace the outline of the caul on each sheet. **D** Use a sharp knife and straightedge cut the excess away.

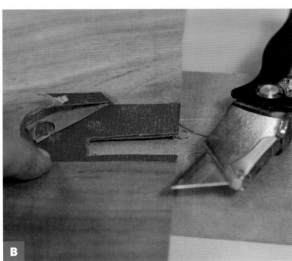

GLUE THE SHOW VENEERS TO THE CORE

Do another dry rehearsal and gather all items needed for the final pressing.  Place the inner show veneer with the good side down and tack it to the form using blue masking tape. Spread glue on the inside of the core and drop it on top of the form. Spread glue over the outer face and lay the outer veneer, good side up, onto the sandwich. Add the top caul, tape it down with two strips of packing tape, and slip it all into the vacuum bag to be pressed.

NOTE You can also do another "mini pressing" if you feel the glue will set before everything is in the bag. As before, press one veneer for 45 minutes, then the other for at least six hours.  Make another pair of props that will also act as supports for the assembly of the wall panel when it comes out of the bag. Make sure to cover it with a soft material.

PREPARE THE PANEL FOR EDGING

After the panel is fully cured, it needs to be cleaned up and prepped for edging. A simple and safe method is to create a sled for the tablesaw to trim it up.  Arrange two pieces of MDF centered one on top of the other with the top piece narrow enough to let the panel overhang it. 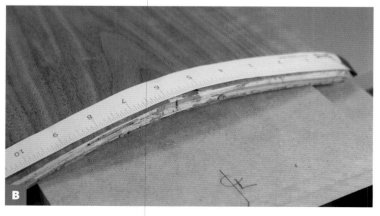 Use a flexible tape measure, like those from a fabric store, to double-check the centering lines on the panel.

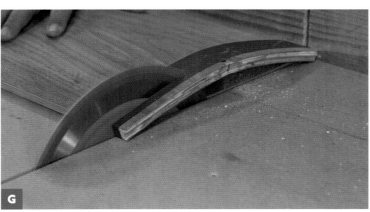

C Burnish blue masking tape onto the cut lines along the length of the edges and use a screw and a washer to temporarily attach the panel to the sled through the centering holes. Tighten just enough to hold both ends of the panel firmly during the cut, but not too much to deform the curve. **D** To determine the angle of the tablesaw, use your eyes and a sliding bevel gauge. Perfection is not necessary. **E** For more accuracy, use a digital angle finder. **F** Tilt the blade on the saw and carefully cut off the ends along with part of the sled. Turn it around, adjust the fence for an even width from center, and cut once more. **G** A crosscut sled works perfectly on the ends.

APPLY THE EDGING TO TOP & BOTTOM

A To cap off the exposed core, use what you like. I chose imbuia for contrast. Mill up some ⅛"-thick pieces that are wide enough and long enough for the top and bottom as well as the vertical edges. **B** Use clamps and cauls to glue the top and bottom first. **C** Clean them up when cured with a spokeshave. **D** You could use a block planes, files, or sandpaper. **E** Flush up both ends, being careful not to cut into the veneer. The vertical edging will cover the top and bottom edges.

APPLY THE EDGING TO THE SIDES

A Repeat the edging process on the vertical edges. **B** Clean up with a block plane and sandpaper. **C** This is a great incentive for using white glue. When flushing the edges with a block plane, white glue shavings in the edging material indicate it's time to slow down because you're getting close.

REPAIRING A CHIPPED EDGE

A One repair that can be made seamlessly is a chipped edge. **B** Apply white glue. **C** Cover with masking tape. If you've lost the piece that chipped off, it's easy to replace it with another. **D** Sanding and a good finish will render this repair invisible.

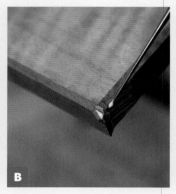

SAND THE PANEL

A To clean the outside of the panel, a sander with a secondary soft pad will work great. Go gently and remember you only have so much veneer to work with. Do a general cleaning with 150 or 180 grit, then switch to handsanding up to 220 grit. **B** Attack small scratches and problem areas with handsanding. **C** For the inside, handsanding does the trick. Use the custom sanding blocks.

MAKE A SHELF FOR THE PANEL

Adding a small shelf that matches the piece provides a nice space for keys or a phone. Use the rib template to create a pleasing, matching shape. **A** A trick to help select the right section from a veneer sheet (or solid wood) is to create a cardboard window. To find a piece of veneer with a slight curve that matches the panel curve, simply position the window over the veneer and cut a piece larger than needed. Use ½"-thick MDF and press the shelf in a vacuum bag, your homemade press, or with a veneer hammer. Keep the cut-offs from the shelf veneer to edge. **B** Decide the shelf location, remembering the bottom of the panel doesn't touch the floor. Mark the location with tape and mark both the center and parallel lines from the bottom of the panel. **C** After making a shelf template, use light passes with a disk sander to make it fit the curve at the taped location on the panel. **D** Use double-sided tape to attach the template to the shelf stock and cut close to it on a bandsaw. **E** Use a bearing pattern router bit to finish shaping it.

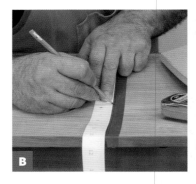

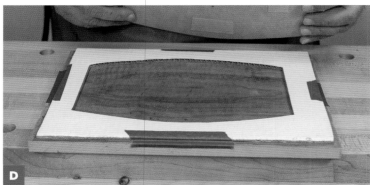

EDGE THE SHELF

A Using white glue, cauls, and clamps, attach the edging to all sides except the back. **B** Address the ends first by cutting off the excess. **C** Then, clean them up with a file. **D** Attach the front edging with a band clamp and ⅛"-thick pieces of hardboard cauls. Clean it all up once the glue has cured.

MAKE THE FRENCH CLEAT FOR HANGING

The *H* frame is basically a pair of cleats sandwiched between two legs and attached to the wall. The cleats on the back of the curved panel hook into the cleats on the *H* frame.  **A** To make the cleats for the back of the panel, profile them to the curve using the rib template and a spindle sander. Make the cleats out of 1" stock. **B** The other half of the French cleat will reside in the *H* frame attached to the wall with the resting surfaces for the panel beveled to approximately 9°. The wall mounted frame is 50" tall and 4½" wide. It makes the panel "float" away from the wall just enough for a pleasing profile and shadow line. **C** To attach the French cleat to the back, find the center and make sure that it is parallel to the sides. Use masking tape to avoid cleaning up pencil lines and scuffs later on. **D** Drill two holes in the French cleat for dowels and then use those as guides to drill into the back of the panel.

E Center the block on the back of the curved piece. Don't trust a masking tape depth stop for this; you'll poke through. Make your own positive-depth stop with a piece of hardwood drilled with the next size larger bit. **F** Set the bit deep enough and make the block long enough to only push three-quarters of the way into the panel. If using a brad-point bit, be aware of that point. **G** Insert dowels and add glue. **H** Secure the cleat onto the back of the panel. Repeat for the second one.

ATTACH THE SHELF

A Drill a pilot hole through the front of the panel and through the center of the shelf. **B** Countersink this hole on the back and then drive a screw into the shelf from behind the panel. **C** Using careful measurements, countersink and drive two more screws from behind. **NOTE** Add one or two drops of thin cyanoacrylate glue to the screw holes in the shelf to stiffen up the screws and prevent stripping. The nature of the curve and the screws have a surprising amount of power to hold the shelf in place. Add a small bracket underneath as a support if you're worried about it breaking off under a heavy load.

ATTACH THE MIRROR

D Use solid stock and, while the pieces are still square, cut kerfs into the pieces as thick as the mirror. **E** Use the shape of the curve to give it a pleasing detail. Carefully center the brackets above the shelf and drive one screw each from the rear of the panel into the brackets.

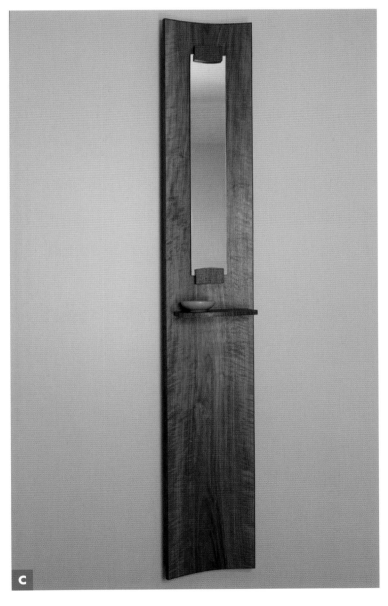

FINISH THE PANEL

A Clean up any scuff marks, scratches, or pencil lines in preparation of applying the finish separately to each of the panel pieces, including the wall cleat *H* frame, the shelf, and the mirror clips. **B** Apply the finish to the panel and allow everything to dry. Re-attach the shelf and mirror brackets. After the brackets are secure, hang the panel by mounting the *H* frame to the wall and then seating the French cleats into position. **C** Take a step back and admire your finished panel.

WRAPPING UP

As mentioned earlier, bending wood like this is accurate, reliable, and repeatable. And, with the backer veneer in place, the projects are strong and stable. If you built the Curved Wall Panel, you'll agree it's not as hard as it looks, and I sincerely hope it sets you on a path to building more curved projects.

WHERE TO FROM HERE?

Just Keep Veneering...

If you've ventured through the book and have made it this far, my sincere hope is that, like myself and many others, you've discovered veneering is an exciting and very worthwhile woodworking technique. It's also a very fun way to work with wood. At the very least, I hope any hesitation or negative thoughts you've harbored about veneering have vanished.

Much like any learning process, what you do with the information after the lessons have ended is the real journey. Personally, when it comes to veneering and woodworking (and life, too, I guess), I never want to stop learning as I explore new and different methods in an effort to improve. There are countless veneers that I've never used that I'd like to learn more about. Right now, while there are a lot of small and odd-shaped veneered "scraps" left over in my shop from veneer projects, there are so many more to be added through the exploration of different veneers and the building of new, different projects. In the end, I can guarantee that the more you engage with veneer, regardless of what you're making, the better you're going to get.

So, where to from here? Keep playing around with veneer. Make mistakes and just practice, practice, practice. Practice does make perfect, but how about aiming for "pretty good" and just having some fun playing with veneer. There is still so much to learn. If you used this book to dip your toe in the water, well, now you can jump right in. Every time you apply veneer, you're inputting experience to your brain and your hands. Even the mistakes will teach you things that you'll carry forward: you'll get better at putting down the right amount of glue; you'll know when a blade is getting too dull to cut cleanly; you'll know how much larger to size your panel in case things shift. In the end, mistakes won't be a problem because you'll know how to fix them.

Ultimately, I hope the knowledge and skills you've picked up working through the methods and projects of this book will give you a good strong base to fall back on while you push further out into the craft. If you have any interest in marquetry, inlay, and parquetry, I hope you take a course or continue to read about those methods and techniques.

ONE FINAL TECHNIQUE TO CONSIDER

Once a teacher, always a teacher... One final technique to explore as you learn more about veneer is to try cutting your own. While I don't do it as much anymore, I did it fresh out of school and it was a satisfying endeavor.

Occasionally, I would luck out and discover an amazing piece of solid wood; a true diamond in the rough. I'd bring it back to the shop knowing I could I extend its use by turning it into veneers. If you have your bandsaw set up properly and have access to a thickness planer and drum sander, it's very possible for you to do the same.

Tack the wood to a slightly larger board of MDF with hot glue to make your own veneer.

Shop-sawn veneers are typically cut a little thicker, which allows them to be handplaned instead of just sanded. The basic concept in creating your own veneer is to first true up the thickness of the wood. Place a cabinetmaker's triangle on one edge. Tack the sides and end of the wood to a slightly larger board of MDF with hot glue. Cut a slice less than ⅛" on the bandsaw and put it aside. Then, run the piece, with MDF base, through the thickness planer and clean the freshly sawn edge. Go back to the bandsaw and so on until you are just short of the MDF panel. If the hot glue touches the blade, it won't dull it. Finally, run the rough faces of your veneer pieces through a drum sander to smooth them out and make them even thinner. The pieces will generally rip apart in a thickness planer, but not a drum sander. The triangle will help keep the pieces in the same order they came off the plank. If this brief elevator lesson on making your own veneer sparks any interest, research it some more or visit *www.blackwalnutstudio.ca.*

BE AN ACTIVE LEARNER & PASS IT ON

So, back to what's next. Here are a few thoughts. Pick a project that calls for solid wood and integrate veneer into parts of it. Get online, take a look at all the available veneers, and order some. If you're lucky enough to have a local supplier, stop in and rifle through their selection. Don't be shy; talk to the staff and ask questions if you have any. The primary reason I keep shopping at my local wood retailer is the staff. They have so much knowledge about wood and I want to soak it all in. Give yourself a challenge with a different method and interesting project. If you screw it up, don't worry about it. It's all part of the learning process.

And, as you continue to develop your skills, make sure to talk to other woodworkers not only to gain knowledge, but to share it. It's a great feeling and it will pay itself back tenfold. In the end, we're a community, and this woodworking thing, it's not meant to be a secret.

Pass it on...

GLOSSARY

backer veneer
Veneer that is used under other veneers to either cross laminate or build up thickness. Usually very plain, nondescript veneer.

bending form
A form around which veneer can be bent to create curves and nonlinear shapes.

bleed through
When glue seeps through to the show face side of a pressing.

book match
Opening a pair of sequential veneers like a page in a book, revealing a mirror image of each other.

caul
A piece of hardboard, MDF, or bendable ply to help spread clamping pressure, as well as protect delicate surfaces from clamp pads, vacuum netting, etc.

cold creep
A term given to PVA glues since they do not cure rigid, but have a small amount of elasticity.

cook
Veneering slang for pressing a veneer panel, etc., in a vacuum bag.

cross-grain lamination
The process of adhering veneer with the grain running perpendicular to the grain of the substrate.

delamination
When veneer separates from its core.

edging or cap
Veneer or solid wood to cover edges of veneered components.

flip match
Sliding a sequential pair of veneers beside each other, then flipping one 180°.

flitch
A stack of veneer sheets cut from a log and kept in sequence.

glue side/face
The side of the veneer that is glued to the substrate.

jointing veneer
To create a perfect seam between two edges so that they can be joined.

marquetry
Assembly of veneer pieces into a picture.

MDF (medium-density fiberboard)
A manmade material composed of glue and wood chips with a very uniform thickness and texture.

parquetry
Assembly of veneer pieces into a geometric pattern.

plain sliced
Cutting veneer completely across a log. Also known as flat sliced.

quarter sliced
Cutting veneer perpendicular to the growth rings.

raw veneer
Veneer that does not have any paper backing nor adhesive already applied to one side.

rift cut
Cutting veneer at a low angle to the radius of the log.

rotary cut
Cutting veneer off a log, much like pulling paper towels off of a roll.

sand through
Sanding through to the core of a veneered piece.

sequential
Veneers are typically cut, dried, and stored to keep the order with which they came off of the log.

show side/face
The side of veneer that faces up; not the glue side. Also known as the face side.

slip match
Sliding a sequential set of veneers beside each other.

springback
The term for when a curved panel pulls away from its form after removing it from clamps or a vacuum bag.

substrate
The base onto which veneers are glued, such as plywood, MDF, etc. Also known as the core.

APPENDIX

CURVED WALL PANEL BENDING FORM PROJECT PLANS

Use this cut list, rib template, and bending form drawing to complete the bending form for the Curved Wall Panel (page 148).

CUT LIST

QTY	PIECE	MATERIAL	L	W	T
1	Bending form rib template	Plywood	13"	3¾"	½"
28	Bending form ribs	MDF	13"	3¾"	½"
50	Bending form spacers	MDF	2½"	2"	½"
2	Bending form surface and caul	Bendable plywood	72"	12"	5mm
1	Bending form base	MDF	72"	13"	¾"

Bending Form Rib Template

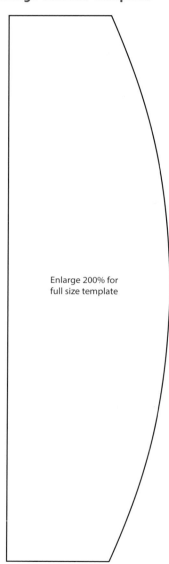

Enlarge 200% for full size template

Bending Form Plan

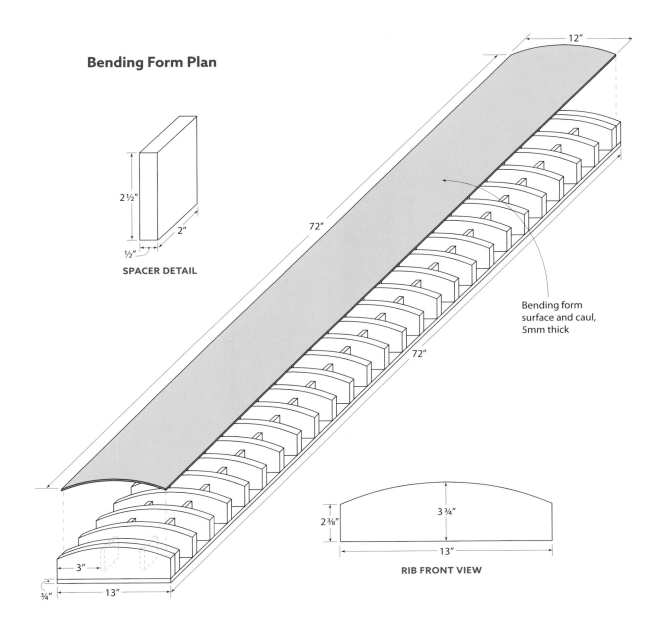

SPACER DETAIL

2½"

2"

½"

72"

72"

Bending form surface and caul, 5mm thick

3"

13"

¾"

RIB FRONT VIEW

3¾"

2⅜"

13"

12"

ABOUT THE AUTHOR

I love working with wood. I also love teaching. What we do isn't a secret; it shouldn't be a secret. I find when I teach that, inevitably, I end up learning something. I never want to stop learning.

I have a personality where I can't do things halfway. When I discovered woodworking early on, I dove quite deep into it. First, it was on my own; then, watching Norm and the New Yankee Workshop, and reading too. I ended up with one of James Krenov's books and eventually found myself at Rosewood Studio.

I initially gravitated heavily toward power tools, then almost completely the other way to hand tools. With time, I found a balance where I do the grunt work with power tools and then spend my energy on refining joints and surfaces with my hands and the tools that they hold.

It has been a great journey so far.

ACKNOWLEDGEMENTS

There are a lot of people to thank. First of all, you for purchasing my book. I also want to thank the academy. I've always wanted to say that. I'm not sure what academy I'm thanking but I heard that on TV and it sounded good.

There are also my instructors, some of whom have become great friends. Ron Barter, Ted Brown, Adrian Ferrazzutti, Michael Fortune, Garrett Hack, Robert Van Norman, and a few more. There are other masters who have influenced me profoundly, including, but not limited to: James Krenov, Sam Maloof, Tage Frid, Norm Abram, and still a few more. Some I have met in person, others I have talked with, and still others I have "met" by reading their books.

Vic Tesolin: I am much richer in life for having you as a friend.

Peter MacSween is a good friend who helped feed my veneer habit.

I want to thank my dad and both my moms. Also Kim, Aida, Seta, Stephen, Mona, Fred, Robert, Kevin, Dan, Alex, Tony, Pat, Mary Anne, Andrea, Raphael, Mike, Terry, Jordan, Bar, Diane, Drew, Hrair, Dexter, Tyson, Scott, George, Pedrum, Ara, Jano, Cherif, Paul, Jessie (Goongie), Brayden (Chubb), Alison, Rolando, Walle, and Banjo. First names only on this last list as they might actually be in the witness protection program or on a most-wanted list somewhere.

Last, there are a countless number of people, including students I have taught, and a few more non-woodworking friends, who have helped or influenced my decisions in woodworking and in life without knowing it.

Thank you all...

INDEX

Note: Page numbers in *italics* indicate projects.

RESOURCES

As a woodworker, you probably know about many of these manufacturers and woodworking retailers, but if you're new to the craft it's helpful to have a list of sources as you seek out your supplies.

A&M Wood Specialty
www.forloversofwood.com

Austin Hardwoods & Hardware
www.austinhardwoodsonline.com

B&B Rare Woods
www.dyed-veneer.com

Bessey Tools
www.bessey.de

Brookside Veneers
www.veneers.com

BT&C Hide Glue
www.toolsforworkingwood.com

Certainly Wood
www.certainlywood.com

CMT
www.cmtorangetools.com

Collins Supply
www.collinssupply.com

Crescent Nicholson Sharp Shear File
www.crescenttool.com

Exotic Woods Inc.
https://exotic-woods.com

Festool
www.festool.com

Freud
www.freudtools.com

GL Reserve
glveneer.com

Gramercy Tools
www.toolsforworkingwood.com

Herzog Veneers, Inc.
www.veneeronline.com

HH-66 Vinyl Cement
www.rhadhesives.com

Highland Woodworking
www.highlandwoodworking.com

Joe Woodworker
www.joewoodworker.com

Johnson Level
www.johnsonlevel.com

Klingspor's Woodworking Shop
www.woodworkingshop.com

Lee Valley Tools
www.leevalleytools.com

Mars Erasers & French Curves
www.staedtler.us/en

Marwood, Inc.
www.marwoodveneer.com

Oakwood Veneer Company
www.oakwoodveneer.com

Old Brown Glue
www.oldbrownglue.com

Peachtree Woodworking Supply
www.ptreeusa.com

Pro Glue Veneer Softener
www.vac-u-clamp.com

Roarockit
www.roarockit.com

Rockler Woodworking & Hardware
www.rockler.com

Sauers & Company Veneers
www.sveneers.com

Shop Fox Clamps
www.woodstockint.com

Super-Soft 2 Veneer Softener
www.veneersupplies.com

Titebond
www.titebond.com

Vacuum Pressing Systems Inc.
www.vacupress.com

Veneer Softener
www.veneersystems.com

Veneer Systems Inc.
www.veneersystems.com

Veneer Tech Craftsman Challenge
www.woodworkingnetwork.com/community/veneer-tech-craftsmans-challenge

Waxalit
www.acmos.com

Weinig USA
www.weinigusa.com

Wiggle Wood®
www.naply.com

WiseWood Veneer Company
www.wisewoodveneer.com

Woodcraft
www.woodcraft.com

Woodcrafters Lumber Sales
www.woodcrafters.us

Woodsmith Store
www.thewoodsmithstore.com

Woodworkers Source
www.woodworkerssource.com

Woodworker's Supply
www.woodworker.com

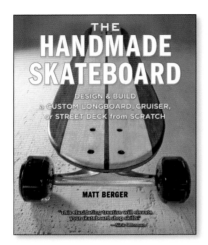
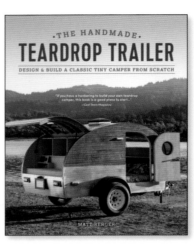
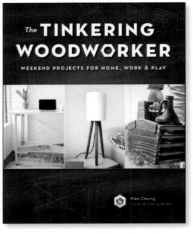
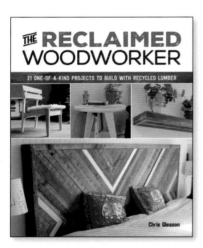
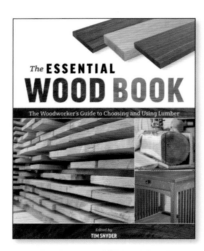

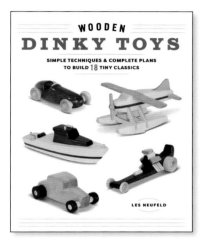
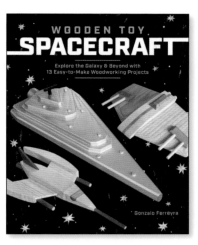
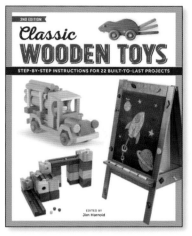

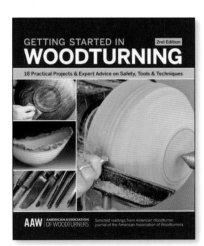
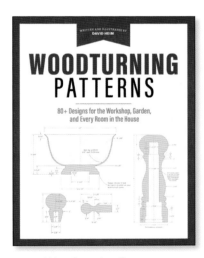

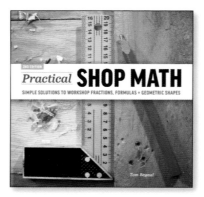